THE FLY FISHERMAN'S GUIDE
to the
Great Smoky Mountains
National Park

THE FLY FISHERMAN'S Guide

TO THE
GREAT SMOKY MOUNTAINS
NATIONAL PARK

H. LEA LAWRENCE

CUMBERLAND HOUSE • *Nashville, Tennessee*

THE FLY FISHERMAN'S GUIDE TO THE
GREAT SMOKY MOUNTAINS NATIONAL PARK
PUBLISHED BY CUMBERLAND HOUSE PUBLISHING, INC.
431 Harding Industrial Drive
Nashville, Tennessee 37211

Copyright © 1998 by H. Lea Lawrence

Photos by Aubrey Watson. Other than the author, the people who appear in
the photographs are Jack Snapp, Stuart Richens, Polly Harrell, and Derek
Porter.

Cover and interior design by Gore Studio, Inc.

Library of Congress Cataloging-in-Publication Data

Lawrence, H. Lea, 1930–
   The fly fisherman's guide to the Great Smoky Mountains National
Park / H. Lea Lawrence.
      p.   cm.
   ISBN: 1-888952-82-2 (pbk.)
   1. Trout fishing—Great Smoky Mountains National Park (N.C. and
Tenn.)—Guidebooks. 2. Fly fishing—Great Smoky Mountains National
Park (N.C. and Tenn.)—Guidebooks. 3. Great Smoky Mountains National
Park (N.C. and Tenn.)—Guidebooks. I. Title.
SH688.U6L38 1998
799.1'757'0976889—dc21   98–16926
                                                              CIP

3 4 5 6 7— 09 08 07 06

*This book is dedicated
to my late father,
Harry C. Lawrence,
who first took me fly fishing in
Smokies streams.*

CONTENTS

ACKNOWLEDGMENTS

I wish to express special thanks and appreciation to Aubrey Watson, who is responsible for most of the color and black-and-white photography in the book; to Jack Snapp, Old Smoky Outfitters, Gatlinburg, Tennessee, for initiating the project and providing invaluable advice and personal assistance in the field; to Paul Ferson of Orvis, Inc., for equipment used in the photography; to Derek Porter, Brevard, North Carolina, for supplying the flies illustrated in the book and for the time spent with me on many streams; to Lance Holland, Marie Williamson, Luther Turpin, and Lester Carrington of Fontana Village Resort, North Carolina, for vital support and services; and to Rick Bivens, James Borawa, Chuck Bradley, Bart Carter, Eric Dennis, David Dickey, Jim Habera, Polly Harrell, Bill Hooks, Earl Huskey, Bob Miller, Jimmy Miller, Bobby Milsaps, Steve Moore, Duane Oliver, Charles Parker, Stuart Richens, Richard Strange, Karen Wade, and Greg Ward.

INTRODUCTION

THE OVERHILL CHEROKEE INDIANS, EARLY INHABITANTS of what is now the Great Smoky Mountains National Park, called this rugged and magnificent cluster of Appalachian mountains with lofty peaks "the land of the eagles and the gods." It was also a land of plenty. The streams teemed with native brook trout, and vast stands of virgin forests held bountiful populations of elk, bison, black bear, white-tailed deer, and wild turkey.

The coming of the white man marked the beginning of this utopia's deterioration. First came the Spanish explorers, ruthless men in search of gold and riches. Later, immigrants from Europe—mostly English and Scottish—began sifting into the region and carving out small homesteads in the remote coves and hidden valleys. They sought privacy and isolation rather than community life, and the wilderness easily absorbed their small numbers. Still, there was an impact because once the first plot of land was cleared for farming, the environment of the Smokies was no longer pristine. It was but a small hint of what was to come.

The events that followed have been well-documented, including wars between whites and Indians, between whites and whites, a steady influx of more and more people, the development of roads and towns, and most significant and damaging, the near-destruction of the virgin forests by logging companies. By the early 1920s huge blocks of timber had already been cut, and there was no end in sight.

In 1923 Mr. and Mrs. Willis P. Davis of Knoxville first conceived the idea of creating a national park in the Smokies. This was quickly accepted by a number of prominent citizens who banded together and mounted a crusade to save what remained of the mountains. Among the group was Horace Kephart, author of the classic book *Our Southern Highlanders,* which details life among the mountain people of the Smokies region.

> A coalition was formed that eventually included thousands of individuals, associations, civic organizations, corporations, state and federal legislative groups, newspapers, businesses, school children, and other interests. It was a battle against enormous odds that required raising huge amounts of money for land purchases and doing battle with powerful lumbering interests racing to harvest as many trees as possible in the face of such opposition. It required years to accomplish, but on June 15, 1934, the Great Smoky Mountains National Park became officially a reality.

Establishment of the park saved more than one hundred thousand acres of old-growth forests, the largest stands in the eastern U.S. Land purchases ultimately brought the total area included within its boundaries to more than eight hundred square miles. Over the years the scarred areas have regenerated and reverted to wilderness, and under the protection of the National Park Service much of the damage done to the flora and fauna has been reversed. This is evidenced by the fact that in 1976 the park was designated by the United Nations Educational, Scientific, and Cultural Organization (UNESCO) as an international Biosphere Reserve because of its great biological diversity. The flora list contains an astounding number of species: more than 1,500 flowering plants, 130 trees, 330 mosses and liverworts, 1,800 fungi, 50 ferns and fern allies, and 230 lichens. Wildlife species are also abundant: 200 birds, 50 mammals, 80 reptiles and amphibians, and 70 fish.

Yet serious problems have arisen that threaten park resources. Air pollution resulting from smog drifting into the mountains from other regions has all but obscured the bluish haze that gave the Smokies their name. In the southeast visibility has declined 60 percent during the last forty-five years, and in the Smokies researchers have determined that views from scenic vistas are impaired by man-made pollution 90 percent of the time. High-elevation streams have little ability to neutralize acids from airborne pollution, which threatens native brook trout populations. Also, scientists have identified ninety species of native park plants that show symptoms of damage from ground-level ozone pollution resulting primarily from automobile exhaust fumes and power plants.

Non-native insects have wrought havoc on park trees, and more problems are anticipated. Fraser fir trees, which occupy the high elevations in the park, have been decimated by the balsam woolly adelgid. A related species, the hemlock woolly adelgid, is approaching the Smokies from the north and is capable of destroying the eastern hemlock trees. Also, the non-native gypsy moth, which defoliates oak, maple, beech, birch, and other deciduous trees, is expected to invade the park soon. As an example of the threat posed, this insect defoliated seventeen thousand acres in the Shenandoah National Park in a single season. Another, the beech scale insect, a European species that has been present in Canada since the late 1800s, was discovered in the park in 1993. In New England the majority of mature American beech trees have been wiped out by beech scale, and since an economically feasible treatment has yet to be discovered, the Smokies' beech trees could face the same kind of devastation.

While over the years more than three hundred species of non-native plants have invaded the Smoky Mountains, there are five particular species that pose the most serious threats to native flora: kudzu, mimosa, Oriental bittersweet, wisteria, and princess trees. The National Park Service is using a grant from the Natural Resource Preservation Program to accelerate its program aimed at suppressing and eradicating them. Other exotics such as privet and Japanese honeysuckle may eventually be added to the list.

Exotic animal species are less prevalent, and the only one to cause extensive damage is the wild hog, sometimes referred to as wild boar. The first of these exotic animals was brought into the mountains in 1912 from Europe, although the hunting preserve on which they were placed was not on land now occupied by the park. They soon escaped the penned areas on the preserve and began interbreeding with free-roaming domestic hogs owned by the mountain people. No doubt some of these infiltrated the park early on, but biologists believe that the main invasion occurred in 1940 with animals from a North Carolina game farm.

Wild hogs do various kinds of damage: They root and furrow the forest floor and damage and destroy native plants, and their appetite includes small mammals, bird eggs, salamanders, snakes, and snails. They are also constantly in competition with black bears for mast crops. One of the worst sins the hogs have committed is the contamination of virtually every spring and stream in the park by wallowing and defecating in the water. Control measures have intensified since 1977, and over 6,500 hogs have been removed by shooting and trapping. Although it is unlikely the hogs can be completely eliminated, ongoing control efforts are required to keep the population at a low level.

Despite these environmental problems, the Great Smoky Mountains National Park remains a paradise for trout fishermen unparalleled anywhere in the eastern United States. It is rugged wilderness country with a broad offering of opportunities for the fisherman. Within its boundaries are more than three hundred fishable streams with a total length of over seven hundred miles. They vary in size from tiny branches narrow enough to step across to broad rivers. Except for the flow on the lower reaches of some of the larger waters, most are fast, tumbling, cascading streams descending rapidly from the backbone of the Smokies, which has sixteen peaks over six thousand feet high within the park. The headwaters of many of the principal watersheds originate well above the five-thousand-foot level and may lose more than two thousand feet in elevation by the time they exit the park boundary.

Because this is a book about fly fishing for trout, the emphasis will be on this resource. The author has made an effort to include all of the information, instructions, and advice required to locate and enjoy whatever type of angling experience one needs to satisfy his or her dreams and desires. A fishing trip in the park can be as easy or as challenging as one wishes to make it. Many waters can be reached within a few steps from an automobile, others by a short walk, and a few by boat. Then there are the numerous remote, high-elevation streams that require lengthy hikes to reach but which offer wonderful isolation and privacy.

Good luck and happy fishing!

THE FLY FISHERMAN'S GUIDE
to the
Great Smoky Mountains
National Park

The majority of park streams are small, yet many of them afford excellent fishing opportunities.

1

Information and Services

LOCATION AND ACCESS

THE GREAT SMOKY MOUNTAINS NATIONAL PARK
sits astride the Tennessee/North Carolina border, with its
acreage nearly evenly divided between the two states. On
the North Carolina side, parts of Haywood and Swain counties
are included, and parts of Cocke, Sevier, and Blount counties
on the Tennessee side. From the standpoint of its position in
the eastern U.S., a line drawn from the southern shore of Lake
Erie near Cleveland, Ohio, to the northern coast of the Gulf of
Mexico would place it at about the halfway mark. The park is
also nearly midway between North Carolina's Atlantic coast
and the Mississippi River.

There is only one road through the park: US 441, which
crosses between Gatlinburg, Tennessee, and Cherokee, North
Carolina. However, there are other highways, secondary roads,
and gravel roads that can be used to reach almost all of the
major points of interest. Almost the entire length of the southern part of the park that borders Fontana Lake can be reached
only on foot or by boat. At one time a road was begun that

4 would have made it accessible by auto, but it was halted by environmental forces that preferred to have that part of the park revert to wilderness. The segment that was completed is known as "The Road to Nowhere," which ends in a 1,200-foot tunnel not far from Bryson City.

Access points in Tennessee are Gatlinburg and Townsend. The easiest access from the north is by exiting I-40 east of Knoxville at exit 407 (TN 66) and following it south to Sevierville, then taking US 441 through Pigeon Forge to Gatlinburg. There are several alternate routes: (1) From the west, a few miles from Kingston exit I-40 onto US 321 and go through Maryville, Townsend, and Pigeon Forge. Near Townsend, just beyond the junction of US 321 and TN 73, turn right to reach the Cades Cove Loop Road. A left turn follows TN 73 along the Little River Road to the NPS Sugarlands Visitor Center near Gatlinburg. (2) From the east, take I-40 toward Asheville after it splits from I-81 and exit on US 411 to the right, following it to Sevierville and on to Gatlinburg, or exit on US 321 and follow it through Cosby and on to Gatlinburg. The latter route parallels the park boundary for much of the distance.

From Chattanooga take I-75 north, exit on US 321, and drive through Maryville, Townsend, and Pigeon Forge. US 321 also skirts the park boundary from Gatlinburg to Cosby.

To reach the North Carolina side of the mountains from Tennessee from the western end of the park, take US 129 at its junction with US 411 south of Maryville. From the eastern end take I-40 toward Asheville, then exit at US 276 to US 19, turn left onto US 19 and follow through Maggie Valley, Cherokee, and Bryson City. A few miles beyond Bryson City on US 19 and US 74, turn right onto NC 28 and proceed to Fontana Village.

The Great Smoky Mountains National Park is open year around, and there is no admission fee. In the winter it is not unusual for US 441 and other roads within the park to be temporarily closed due to heavy snow.

According to what part of the park visiting fly fishermen have targeted, the best places to use as headquarters in Tennessee are: Gatlinburg, Pigeon Forge, Townsend, and Newport; in North Carolina: Fontana Village, Bryson City, Cherokee, Waynesville, and Maggie Valley.

FISHING

Fishing is allowed year around in the open waters, and those possessing either a Tennessee or North Carolina license are permitted to fish anywhere in the park. In Tennessee residents and nonresidents age thirteen and older need a license. The exemption is residents who were sixty-five prior to March 1 of the current year. These persons require only proof of age and Tennessee residence. In North Carolina residents and nonresidents age sixteen and older need a license. Residents age seventy and older may obtain a special license from the state. Persons under sixteen in North Carolina and under thirteen in Tennessee are entitled to the adult daily creel and possession limits and are subject to all other regulations. Licenses are not available at the visitor centers and must be purchased in the nearby towns. No trout stamp is required.

Following are some basic rules for fishing the park:

■ Fishing is allowed from a half hour before sunrise to a half hour after official sunset.

These information and registration units are placed at strategic locations such as trailheads and campgrounds.

- Five rainbow or brown trout are allowed each day in possession, regardless of whether they are fresh, stored in an ice chest, or otherwise preserved. The combined total must not exceed five fish. A person must stop fishing immediately after obtaining a limit.
- The possession of brook trout is prohibited.
- The basic rules require the use of only one hand-held rod, using artificial lures or flies with a single hook. The use of any form of fish bait or liquid scent other than artificial flies or lures on any park streams while in possession of fishing tackle is prohibited.
- Prohibited baits include, but are not limited to, minnows (live or preserved), worms, corn, cheese, bread, salmon eggs, pork rinds, liquid scents, and natural baits found along the streams.
- The use of double, treble, or gang hooks is prohibited on all waters.
- Fishing tackle and equipment, including creels and fish in possession, are subject to inspection by authorized personnel.

INFORMATION SOURCES

Anglers planning a trip to the park can obtain much of the necessary information in advance by contacting: Superintendent, Great Smoky Mountains National Park, 107 Park Headquarters Road, Gatlinburg, TN 37738, (423) 436-1200. Another excellent source is: Great Smoky Mountains Natural History Association (GSMNHA), 115 Park Headquarters Road, Gatlinburg, TN 37738, (423) 436-7318. A nonprofit organization that assists the National Park Service in educational and scientific projects, GSMNHA also operates bookstores at the park's Sugarlands Visitor Center two miles south of Gatlinburg, at Oconaluftee Visitor Center four miles north of Cherokee, and at Cades Cove Visitor Center (which is closed during the winter months). A brochure listing all of the publications sold by the GSMNHA is available at no cost, and phone orders are accepted.

Guided fishing trips for individuals or groups to any of the streams in the park must be conducted by operators licensed by the park. A list of these is available upon request. The park also offers periodic fly fishing instruction courses at the Sugarlands Visitor Center, conducted by Jack Snapp, a licensed guide and owner of Old Smoky Outfitters, P.O. Box 488, Gatlinburg, TN 37738, (423) 430-1936.

Maps are especially important to fishermen, and the sources listed above can supply everything from basic maps to the USGS quadrangles that apply to all portions of the park. Since access to many of the streams in the park is on foot, it is important to have a reliable trail guide. One of the best available is *Hiking Trails of the Smokies,* a pocket-size guide published by GSMNHA that is up-to-date and highly reliable. What makes it a must for serious fly fishermen, particularly backpackers and backcountry campers, is that in addition to listing all of the major trails, it contains details on trails to remote high-elevation streams not shown on most maps. This book also contains a wealth of information on the environment and historical facts about many of the locations through which the trails pass.

GSMNHA bookstores offer other guides including: *The Best of the Great Smoky Mountains: A Hiker's Guide to Trails and Attractions; Time Well Spent: Family Hiking in the Smokies; Hiking in the Great Smokies; The Two-Ounce Backpacker: A Problem-Solving Manual for Use in the Wilds; Appalachian Trail Guide to Tennessee & North Carolina;* and several hikers' packets that include both books and maps. These can be obtained at the park's visitor centers or by ordering by phone from the GSMNHA at (423) 436-7318.

SERVICES

Within the park there is only one place that offers meals and lodging: LeConte Lodge atop Mount LeConte, which is accessible only by trails and open from mid-March through mid-November. Also, due to its popularity, reservations must be made up to a year or more in advance. However, from a fly fisherman's standpoint, this isn't a practical location anyway since it isn't within close proximity to any streams. For those who prefer locations that offer full services such as motel or hotel lodging, restaurants, grocery stores, and other conveniences, the park is surrounded by cities and towns that can serve as headquarters. Those closest to the park on the Tennessee side are Gatlinburg, Pigeon Forge, Townsend, and Cosby, but Sevierville, Maryville, Knoxville, and Newport are within reasonable distance. In North Carolina Fontana Village, Bryson City, Cherokee, and Maggie Valley are nearest, with Asheville, Waynesville, and Sylva as other choices. There are commercial airports at Chattanooga, Knoxville, and Asheville and airports capable of handling private aircraft at Gatlinburg, Sevierville, Pigeon Forge, and Newport.

It is important to remember that from spring through late fall there is no significant break in heavy flow of visitors to the

10 Smokies, and assuring lodgings in most of the towns close to the park requires obtaining reservations well in advance of a trip.

CAMPING

There are ten "drive to" campgrounds throughout the park maintained by the National Park Service. The facilities include tent sites, some trailer spaces, firepits, tables, restrooms, and water. No RV hookups or showers are provided. Reservations are required at some, while others are on a first come, first served basis. There are also variations in the length of stay permitted.

Additionally, there are ninety-eight backcountry campsites at eleven different areas and eighteen trail shelters, all of which require reservations and which have specific requirements for their use.

The rules and regulations for the maintained campgrounds, backcountry campsites, and trail shelters are complex and too lengthy to list here. They are covered in more detail in chapter six. Additionally, *The Great Smoky Mountains Trail Map* (part of which is located in the back of this book) provides this information. It is available at no cost from the National Park Service at the visitor centers or by mail.

2

Trout of the Smokies

IT MIGHT BE LOGICAL TO ASSUME THAT HAD THE activities of man not dramatically altered the habitat of the Great Smoky Mountains, brook trout would still be the predominant—and possibly the only—species of trout present.

That didn't happen, though. Changes in the mountain environment began with the arrival of the first settlers, although this had only a minor overall effect on the brook trout population as compared with the massive destruction resulting from the intensive logging that began in the early 1900s. The net result of these practices was the removal of the canopy from streams, the increase in water temperature, and the influx of silt through runoff. The brookies had no alternative but to retreat to headwater streams where some cover remained.

Rick Bivens, a fisheries biologist for the Tennessee Wildlife Resources Agency who has done extensive studies on brook trout, says before these operations began the species were believed to occupy 421 miles of the streams now included within park boundaries. By the time the park was established in 1934 brook trout had disappeared from more than 158 miles of these waters. A survey by park fisheries biologists in the 1950s showed an additional thirty-eight-mile decline, and more recently (1980) it was determined that there was another 101-

There are big waters on rivers on both the Tennessee and North Carolina sides of the park. The Little River and Oconaluftee are two examples.

mile loss, bringing the total to 70 percent elimination from their original range.

Stephen E. Moore, park fisheries biologist, reported in his 1993 Fisheries Management Plan that prior to 1934 the major factors responsible for the decline of brook trout were obvious: approximately 80 percent of the area was logged, resulting in the loss of approximately 40 percent of the native brook trout due to this commercial activity. The practices included the use of splash dams, the building of logging railroads, brush clearing, fires, and exploitative fishing practices.

Because of the demand for recreational angling in the wake of this decline in brook trout opportunity, the logging companies and well-intentioned individuals began stocking rainbow trout in streams that would eventually be within park boundaries. The latter was done in an effort to provide fishing opportunity in waters where brook trout had vanished.

The problems posed by the stocking of rainbow trout weren't immediately apparent, and Moore says even after the park was established, park managers initially held the belief that as reforestation of the mountains proceeded, the brook trout range would be restored and the species would again predominate. Instead, from the beginning rainbow trout became firmly established in all but the higher-elevation streams and eventually began invading these waters also. As brook trout range continued to decrease in size, the range of rainbow trout expanded.

Another problem arose when brown trout started appearing in park waters. Moore's report indicates the only recorded stocking of this species was in the Oconaluftee River in 1965, but there were other sources over which park rangers had no control. One was the migration of brown trout resulting from stocking programs by state agencies in perimeter waters. The

14   other was the unofficial and illegal stockings by individuals. Today, browns are present in all but two of the watersheds, and there's no guarantee they won't eventually invade them also. On the other hand, rainbows are present in all park waters except for a few high-elevation streams.

In 1984 a National Park Service study by Alston, West, MacKenzie, and McKinney showed rainbow trout to be the dominant species (being found in 80 percent of the streams in the park) with brown trout the second most important with self-sustaining populations primarily below 2,700 feet in elevation. Since that time these populations have continued to increase and are continually being reported in new locations in smaller headwater streams.

The stocking of rainbow trout continued after the park was established, but the practice was gradually reduced and finally discontinued in 1975. However, during this stocking period another "exotic" was inadvertently introduced after an effort to restore native brook trout populations in many of the streams failed. The plan was to produce brook trout in hatcheries using local brood stock. When this didn't work, managers imported northern hatchery strains of brook trout. Eventually, over eighty thousand were stocked throughout the park.

Even at the outset of this stocking program, there were both local anglers and biologists who believed that brook trout native to the Smokies were a different species than those from northern waters. Over the years scientific studies came down on both sides of the controversy. However, through the use of DNA technology, it has been proven that the Appalachian brook trout is indeed a separate strain.

Rather than wait for official confirmation that the southern brook trout were unique, in 1983 the National Park Service hired a permanent fishery biologist for the Smokies. Soon afterward the Native Brook Trout Restoration Program was initiated, and since then a great deal of progress has been made in identifying, monitoring, and protecting those locations where they survive. It was known through stocking records that some streams, mostly those at high elevations, had never been stocked with the northern strain. When field research got underway, more of the high-elevation waters were inventoried. At this point biologists discovered many more streams and portions of streams holding noncontaminated native brook trout. Some were also found to contain rainbows, which were removed by electroshocking and reintroduced farther downstream.

One hindering factor in the protection of native brook trout is that park policy prohibits the use of man-made barriers such as weir dams or other obstacles to prevent the intrusion of rainbows and browns into native brook trout waters. This leaves waterfalls at least eight feet high or cascades as the only natural features to depend upon. However, in some instances these so-called "barriers" are rendered ineffective by high waters, while some cascades are a natural playground for wild rainbows.

There is reason for optimism, though. Brook trout restoration efforts initiated in 1976 using backpack electrofishing techniques in the Great Smoky Mountains National Park resulted in two streams being restored to brook trout. This makes four since 1991. Thanks to volunteer labor and funding from groups like Trout Unlimited, National Fish and Wildlife Federation, Tennessee Technological University, University of Tennessee, Friends of the Great Smoky Mountains, Tennessee Wildlife Resources Agency, and North Carolina Wildlife Resources Commission, efforts are underway to restore two additional streams.

With more than seven hundred miles of trout water scattered throughout the eight hundred square miles of park lands, it's not difficult to find privacy and solitude.

Field surveys from 1992 to the present also provide reason for hope. Rainbow trout encroachment (upstream movement) has slowed or stopped in some streams but continued slowly in others. In a few streams, brook trout have been found farther downstream than reported in the 1970s. Reasons for these changes are not clear but may be related to forest age or increased acid deposition. Further research and management studies will hopefully provide additional insights into this issue.

Also, it has has been determined that southern fish do hybridize with northern stocks. Genetics research has demonstrated that hybridization was not as big a problem as originally thought, because many streams had received only one or two stockings. On the other hand, streams that had numerous stockings show a much higher degree of hybridization.

The park brook trout program is ongoing, and given adequate funding, fisheries biologists hope restoration of their native range could someday result in anglers again being allowed to fish for brook trout in more of the streams now off-limits. The park's management plan identifies seventeen additional streams for brook trout restoration efforts. The majority of these are larger mid-elevation streams with natural barriers that had rainbow trout stocked in them in the 1920s and 1930s. If successful, this ambitious effort will ensure that native brook trout are protected and preserved for future generations.

There are a number of environmental factors posing threats, some of which could ultimately be insurmountable. Global warming could cause water temperatures to increase beyond the levels of tolerance for some fish and other species. The ongoing destruction of trees in both the higher and lower elevations by exotic insects and diseases threatens the watersheds as well as the overall ecology of the Smokies. Also, sulfates and nitrates deposited by precipitation are harmful.

The park brook trout program is ongoing, and given adequate funding fisheries biologists hope restoration of their native range could someday result in anglers again being allowed to fish for brook trout in some of the streams now off limits. It would be less difficult if the task involved only management of the species, but this isn't the case. There are a number of environmental factors posing threats, some of which may ultimately prove to be insurmountable. Global warming could cause water temperatures to increase beyond the levels of tolerance for some fish and other aquatic species. The ongoing destruction of trees in both the higher and lower elevations by exotic insects and diseases seriously threatens the watersheds, as well as the overall ecology of the Smokies. And in some locations stream acidity levels are increasing due to leaching from Anakeesta outcrops and from carbonic acid deposited by precipitation.

The *Restricted Waters* map in the back of the book shows the locations of the restricted brook trout waters; you may refer to it as you read the following:

North Carolina: (1) Gunter Creek at the first trail crossing on Gunter at 3,240-feet elevation; (2) Big Creek and Yellow Creek at their junction; (3) McGinty Creek at its confluence with Swallow Fork; (4) Correll Branch at the junction with Little Cataloochee Creek; (5) Lost Bottom Creek at its confluence with Panther Creek at 3,280-feet elevation; (6) Bunches Creek at the park boundary; (7) Stillwell Creek at the park boundary; (8) Straight Fork and Balsam Corner Creek at their common junction; (9) Raven Fork at Big Pool, which is the confluence of Left Fork, Middle Fork, and Right Fork (also known as Three Forks); (10) Enloe Creek at the junction with

Raven Fork; (11) Taywa Creek at its confluence with Bradley Fork; (12) Chasm Prong and Gulf Prong at their common junction on Bradley Fork; (13) Sahlee Creek at its confluence with Deep Creek; (14) Noland Creek and Salola Branch at their confluence; (15) Huggins Creek (tributary of Forney Creek) at the cascade at 3,700-feet elevation; (16) Hazel Creek at the base of Hazel Creek Cascades; (17) Walkers Prong at the falls at 3,400-feet elevation; (18) Defeat Branch at its junction with Bone Valley Creek; (19) Gunna Creek (tributary to Eagle Creek) at trail crossing at 3,280-feet elevation.

Tennessee: (20) Sams Creek at the confluence of Thunderhead Prong; (21) Marks Creek at the falls at 2,600-feet elevation; (22) Lynn Camp Prong at Campsite 28 (Marks Cove) at 3,490-feet elevation (1.6 miles); (23) Indian Flats Prong where the Middle Prong Trail crosses at 2,960-feet elevation; (24) Meigs Creek at its confluence with Little River; (25) Fish Camp Prong and Goshen Creek at their common junction; (26) Little River and Grouse Creek at their common junction; (27) Road Prong at its confluence with West Prong of the Little Pigeon River; (28) Buck Fork and Eagle Rocks Prong at their common junction; (29) Dunns Creek at the park boundary; (30) Indian Camp Creek at the park boundary; (31) Greenbrier Creek (Little Creek) at the park boundary; (32) Toms Creek at its junction with Cosby Creek; (33) Cosby Creek where Low Gap Trail crosses the stream; (34) Rock Creek at its junction with Cosby Creek; (35) Spruce Flats Creek at its confluence with Middle Prong of Little River; (36) Meigs Post at its confluence with Little River.

Big waters allow for plenty of casting room, and this is where longer rods and weight-forward lines are needed.

3

Basic Equipment, Knots, Accessories, and Safety Tips

ONE OF THE PRINCIPAL THINGS TO KEEP IN MIND when choosing basic equipment for fishing the Smokies is that the majority of streams are small; there are some that could be described as tiny. A few are called rivers, but even these are fairly moderate in size, especially by western standards.

This means the selection of tackle for use on Smokies streams is extremely important, and it's likely that a single outfit won't be suitable for all situations and conditions encountered. Chances are you'll want one for use on open water and another for little waters where short casts are required.

For example, there's a great difference in the kind of tackle suited for the larger streams, where more line can be worked and longer casts are possible, and the tackle required to efficiently fish the little tributaries or high-elevation streams. On these diminutive waters short casts are the rule most of the time because often the angler is operating in extremely close quarters and must place the fly accurately into small, hard-to-reach pockets under overhanging limbs or shrubs. Sometimes, when fishing tight spots overgrown with vegetation, it's necessary to use a bow-and-arrow cast or to crawl in and dabble a fly with only a couple of feet of leader out beyond the rod tip.

Compact pack rods of 5 1/2- to 7-foot lengths are popular among those who like to hike into the backcountry.

Obviously, these facts are critical in the matter of selecting rods, reels, line, and leaders. They will influence choices of other items too, but the basic elements are the most important to consider initially. From a monetary standpoint, the main emphasis should be placed on the rod and line. These two tools work much harder on a stream during the day than the reel, the principal purpose of which is only to store line.

It's not as simple as going out and buying the outfits. Equipment has to be carefully coordinated in terms of weight, length, and size in order to balance and perform satisfactorily. Mismatched tackle causes most of the problems encountered by novice anglers. It's a handicap that can be avoided by purchasing gear from either a shop that specializes in fly fishing equipment or one of the top mail-order companies offering balanced outfits, or by getting advice from an experienced fly caster. Also, attending a fly fishing school can be a big advantage. It can cut learning time from days or months to a few days, and it's well worth the cost involved.

RODS

Because of the great diversity in the size and types of fishing waters in the park, it's not possible to select one rod that will be right for all situations. At places where the water is no more than a couple of yards wide, a 5 1/2- to 6 1/2-foot backpack rod may be perfect. Others sites might be many times that width and require a much longer rod for suitable performance. The ideal solution would be for anglers to have a rod specific to every kind of water, but not many can afford such a luxury. Instead, if you plan to fish a variety of water types and

24

sizes, the best idea is to pick a rod that will work well in the widest variety of circumstances.

Generally speaking, the rods practical for most Smokies waters are those in the 7- to 8-foot lengths. The action and length may vary according to the angler's preference of fishing methods. Dry fly fishermen are more concerned with rod action than with length, while nymph fishermen want a longer rod to better control line in a drift and for mending ability. These are fairly minor differences, however, and finding a rod that's adequate for both purposes isn't really a problem.

Most fly rods today are made of graphite, which is tough, durable, and impervious to the elements. It has a higher strength-to-weight ratio, and rods made of graphite may weigh one to three ounces less than those made of other materials. Also, the responsiveness and "feel" of graphite rods is highly desirable. Since it appeared on the scene, an overwhelming number of trout fishermen now prefer it over split bamboo and fiberglass. The latter material has almost disappeared from rod making, but this is not true of split bamboo. While in the minority, there are some anglers who are still staunchly loyal to split bamboo because of tradition and appreciation of fine craftsmanship.

In the area of cost, a good graphite rod can be bought for under $125, but it's possible to pay up to $600 for the more exclusive models. Split bamboo rods begin in the neighborhood of $450 and continue on up to $1,500 and beyond for custom-built models.

REELS

The single-action fly reel is the choice in most fly fishing environments today, particularly for the kinds of conditions encountered in the Smokies, since its primary function is simply for line storage. Reels are available in a number of styles, with the ventilated spool models favored due to weight and noise reduction.

Most modern fly reels are made of aluminum that, in addition to being a lightweight material, is resistant to corrosion. Within the aluminum reel family there are cast-aluminum reels and those machined from bar stock. The principal difference is in price, with the cast-aluminum models selling for about half the cost of bar-stock reels. Also, bar-stock reels are structurally more stable, although this isn't a factor of which most anglers are aware. What's most important is durability, and reels that are beefed up on the exterior with baked enamel finishes of Teflon coating are good choices.

Better quality reels are equipped with drag systems designed to slow down long, hard runs by big fish. In the park streams this situation will rarely occur, so drag systems aren't an important factor in choosing a reel for our purposes.

As with rods, there's a wide range of prices in reels, with some models costing up to four hundred dollars. Functionally, though, there's virtually no difference.

Simply put, you can't beat a reasonably priced, single-action, spring-and-pawl fly reel with its lightweight and corrosive-resistant properties for Smokies fishing.

Choosing the best line is essential for attaining maximum performance on the stream.

LINES, LEADERS, AND TIPPETS

Fly lines can be placed in these general categories: (1) numbered by weight from #1 to #16, with the lowest number designating the smallest weight in grains; (2) weight-forward, double-taper, and level (which is rarely used today); and (3) sinking or floating. Within that basic structure are many specialty lines designed for specific purposes, but for the most part they don't apply to the needs of park anglers.

Weighted Lines

Line weight and configuration are very important when fishing Smokies waters due to the predominance of situations in which short casts and roll casts are necessary. All told, #4, #5, and #6 weights are preferable because they permit more versatility. A #5 weight is probably close to ideal since you can cast a variety of fly types with it. A #4 weight is more labor intensive than a #5 weight, and if casting large streamers or weighted nymphs the #5 weight handles them more efficiently and with less effort. Obviously, a #6 weight will handle these bigger flies well too, but the #5 weight remains the best middle-of-the-road choice. It's very easy to roll cast, and with it everything from small, delicate dry flies to streamers can be presented effectively under a wide variety of conditions.

The ultimate in presentation of dry flies is attained by the use of ultralight rods built to handle #2- and #3-weight lines. This can give the angler a special advantage when fishing in very clear or low water conditions where the trout are extremely spooky. Such rods are available in both conventional and travel models.

28   Weight-Forward and Double-Taper Lines

Weight-forward lines are popular in the Smokies—having the belly of the line out quickly is helpful in making short casts and roll casts—but double-taper lines have a particular advantage that doesn't necessarily apply to their function on the water. Because each half of the line is the same, it's really two lines in one. When one end has become worn after a few seasons, reverse it on the spool and you have a new line. This is practical, especially when the cost of a good fly line is considered. (This can be done with level lines also, but very few fishermen use them anymore.)

Sinking Lines

There are sink-tip lines that are useful at certain times of the year, especially for fishermen who remain active in the late fall, winter, and early spring months when trout are in deep water and aren't too active. At such times the offering has to be put almost right on their nose in order to get a strike, and the sinking tip helps streamers and nymphs get down to the level where the trout are holding.

There are three basic types of sinking lines: slow, intermediate, and fast, with the intermediate being the most suitable for Smokies streams and rivers. Try to avoid using sink-tip attachments on the front of your floating line; the hinging effect caused by these rigs makes casting control very difficult. Too, they're unnecessary since the technology now present in the manufacturing of fly lines opts for lines with the sink tip extruded beyond the floating portion.

Note: Nymph fishermen like lines with a brightly colored segment on the forward end that provides high visibility and helps signal subtle strikes that might not otherwise be detected.

Leaders (Tippets)

Smokies trout aren't usually too leader shy, and from the standpoint of being able to place flies accurately on the water, very light tippets should be avoided; it's hard to turn them over suitably on short casts. In most cases 4- to 6-pound test is sufficient. The exception to this is during low water conditions when the fish are easily alarmed and difficult to approach. At these times it's necessary to use long leaders with 6- or 7-pound tippets. In by far the majority of situations, a 7 1/2-foot leader is all that's needed, and when using 5 1/2- to 6 1/2-foot rods even shorter ones are suitable. Naturally, there are instances, especially on bigger waters, where 9-foot leaders are better, but the idea of going beyond that length isn't likely to come to mind.

KNOTS

Knots are the most important connection between the angler and the fish because, regardless of the strength of the line and leader, a poorly tied knot can literally "undo" it all.

Learning the proper knots to use with fly-fishing tackle is a necessary, and probably one of the easiest, part of the whole process of becoming qualified in the sport. In all, there are five basic knots sufficient to cover the needs of park fishermen.

Improved Clinch Knot — TO HOLD TERMINAL TACKLE

This is a good knot for connecting the leader to the fly.

1. Pass the line through the eye of the hook. Double back and make five turns around the standing line.

2. Holding the coils in place, thread the end of the line around through the first loop above the eye, then through the big loop.

3. Hold the tag end and standing line while pulling up the coils. Make sure the coils are in a spiral, not lapping over each other. Slide tightly against the eye.

4. Clip the tag end.

ILLUSTRATIONS COURTESY OF STREN FISHING LINES

Polamar Knot — TO HOLD TERMINAL TACKLE

This knot is equivalent to the Improved Clinch, yet is easier to tie.

1. Double about four inches of line and pass the loop through the eye.

ILLUSTRATIONS COURTESY OF STREN FISHING LINES

Polamar Knot, cont.   TO HOLD TERMINAL TACKLE

2. Let the hook hang loose and tie an overhand knot in the doubled line. Avoid twisting the lines, and don't tighten.

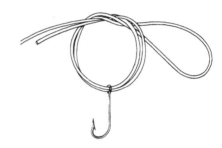

3. Pull the loop of line far enough to pass it over the hook. Make sure the loop passes completely over.

4. Pull both the tag end and the standing line to tighten.

5. Clip the tag end.

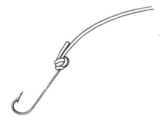

ILLUSTRATIONS COURTESY OF STREN FISHING LINES

Simplified Blood Knot

A LEADER-TO-LEADER KNOT

This knot is used to tie segments of leader together when creating a tapered leader or when adding tippet material.

1. Take the ends of the two strands of leader, tie a simple overhand knot (which you will later clip off), and tighten.

2. Form a loop where the two lines meet with the overhand knot in the loop.

3. Pull one side of the loop down and begin turning it around the standing line. Keep the points where the turns are made open so the turns will gather equally on both sides.

4. After eight to ten turns reach through the center opening and pull the remaining loop (with the overhand knot) through. Keep your finger in this loop so the loop will not spring back.

5. Hold the loop with your teeth, and pull both ends of the line, gathering the turns on each side of the loop.

6. Set the knot by pulling the lines as tight as possible. Tightening the coils will make the loop stand out perpendicular to the line.

7. Clip off the loop and overhand knot close to the newly formed loop.

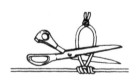

ILLUSTRATIONS COURTESY OF STREN FISHING LINES

Surgeon's End Loop

A LOOP KNOT

Use this knot to tie a loop in the end of a line or leader in order to make a quick attachment.

1. Double the end of the line to form a loop, then tie an overhand knot at the base of the doubled line.

2. Leaving the loop open, bring the doubled line through once more.

3. Hold the standing line and tag end and pull the loop to tighten the knot. You can adjust the loop size by shifting the loose knot before tightening.

4. Clip the tag end.

ILLUSTRATIONS COURTESY OF STREN FISHING LINES

Dropper Loop

This forms a loop in the middle of an otherwise unknotted line, giving you a place to attach a hook, sinker, or fly. Though this is not a strong knot, it is useful with panfish and small saltwater species.

1. Form a loop in the line.

2. Pull one side of the loop down and begin turning it around the standing line. Keep points where turns are made open so turns will gather equally on each side.

3. After eight to ten turns, reach through the center opening and pull the remaining loop through. Keep your finger in this loop so the loop will not spring back.

4. Hold the loop with your teeth and pull both ends of the line, gathering the turns on each side of the loop.

5. Set the knot by pulling the lines as tight as possible. Tightening the coils will make the loop stand out perpendicular to the line.

ILLUSTRATIONS COURTESY OF STREN FISHING LINES

BOOTS, WADERS, AND SHOES 35

First off, it should be noted that felt soles are a must in the park because of the slime that builds up on the freestone rocks and boulders. Nothing—even metal hobnails or cleats— works better in preventing falls. Anglers from outside the region often show up with hip boots or waders with lug-type rubber soles and soon end up experiencing a tumble or a dunking. This doesn't mean new boots or waders have to be purchased, but it does suggest getting an inexpensive felt-sole kit to remedy the problem.

Boots

For the novice to intermediate fly fisherman, hip boots are both sufficient and economical. Most park streams drop abruptly off the mountainsides, and while they're swift, most aren't too deep. When large pools are encountered, it's usually easy to navigate around them. Too, until one has some experience with wading in rapidly moving water, it's best not to get in too deep! There are hip boots available in various kinds of material, both insulated and noninsulated models.

Waders

With regard to full-size waders, neoprene is an excellent material during the months when water temperatures are quite chilly. But in the summer months when the air temperature may be between 80 and 90 degrees and the humidity as high as 80 percent, they're too warm. The perspiration generated will leave the wearer as wet inside the waders as if he or she had fallen in. Also, the abrasion factor should be considered because crawling over rocks and pushing through streamside laurel thickets can quickly ruin a pair of neoprenes. Something else: Neoprenes aren't what you want to tote when walking into remote streams; they're heavy.

What works best for all-around Smokies fishing are waders made of 300-grade or better nylon. These are light and extremely tough and can be expected to last for years. Several companies manufacture them, and they are produced in both chest-high and waist-high versions.

Flyweight stocking-foot waders are a good choice and are available in fabrics that breathe and prevent perspiration from accumulating inside. Those anglers who like to go into remote streams are especially partial to flyweights because they can put the waders in a pack and wear wading shoes to walk in. Once at the stream they can put the waders on and at the end of the day return them to the pack for the walk back out. (There are also very light wading shoes made for this kind of fishing.)

Waders should be tried on to make sure they fit properly. Freedom of movement is necessary for comfort, but they should fit snugly enough to prevent blistering or chafing. This may sound somewhat contradictory, but it's possible to reach a satisfactory compromise. Pay close attention to the feet since, in the case of the boot-foot models, they must be roomy enough to accommodate the socks worn inside, while the stocking-foot models will have socks both inside and out. It's advisable to wear neoprene socks outside over the stocking-foot since they will prevent gravel from getting in between the boot foot and the shoe. The discomfort this causes is one thing, but gravel can also puncture the fabric and cause leaks.

Shoes

During the warm months of May through September many Smokies fishermen abandon hip boots and waders and wear only felt-sole shoes. They're comfortable and allow great ease in movement, and there's no concern about getting in too deep. Light poplin shirts and pants are ideal for this kind of "wet" wading since they air-dry very fast. Backpackers find this method extremely practical; it means there's one less item to carry along.

FLY VESTS AND ACCESSORIES

Vests

There are many fly vests on the market, some in regular length and others shorter for use with chest waders. They are marvels of efficiency when it comes to providing pockets, D-rings, and pouches to hold every kind of item an angler may wish to place inside or out.

A lighter and sometimes more practical alternative to a fly vest is one of the small tackle packs designed specifically for fly fishermen. These can be carried on a strap in a cross-chest fashion or worn around the waist like a fanny pack. They hold all of the things needed for an individual trip, and a rain jacket, water bottle, or other items can be attached to the outside with straps and D-rings. Another advantage is that a tackle pack eliminates the necessity of wearing another garment; vests can get hot in the summertime.

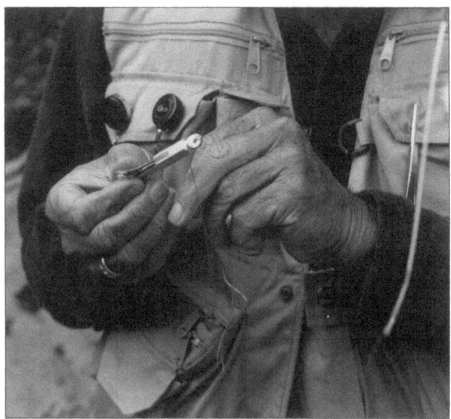

Fly vests work well for carrying essential gear such as fly boxes, leaders, snips, dry fly floatant, and other accessories.

Accessories

In addition to fly boxes, leaders, and tippet material, there are countless accessories with which to load up a fly vest, yet only a dozen or so that can be considered indispensable: forceps; a snip with a built-in needle for cleaning hook eyes (although a pair of nail clippers and a hook point will substitute); liquid, paste, or crystal-powder fly floatant; strike indicators; leader straightener; fly-line cleaner; polarized glasses; a stream thermometer; a small magnifying lens; a nontoxic split-shot dispenser; a waterproof lighter or match box; a small flashlight; a loud whistle or other signaling device; a Swiss army-type knife with screwdriver, pliers, file, scissors, awl, can opener, and other gadgets; and a small first-aid kit.

Additional handy items would include: fly threaders, knot tiers, magnifying eyeglasses, and clip-ons to aid in tying on flies, and sun block and insect repellent.

Stream Thermometers

It's well to elaborate a bit on the stream thermometer, a very valuable accessory. Many fishermen consider it a must since water temperature is the most dependable way to gauge fish activity. For instance, brook trout in the high-altitude streams may begin feeding on nymphs even when the temperature is in the 36- to 40-degree range, and at lower altitudes rainbows and browns are nymphing in 40- to 45-degree water. Dry fly fishermen seldom start to see much surface activity until the water reaches the 57- to 65-degree range. That's ideal for this kind of fishing, yet when temps climb to about the 67-degree level, the water's oxygen-carrying capacity drops and activity slows down. At those times the environment isn't comfortable for trout, especially rainbows, and they adjust by moving upstream or into tributaries where the water is a few degrees cooler. If you're on a stream at low altitude and start seeing 67 degrees or higher on the thermometer, the solution is to hike upstream and keep checking until you locate cooler water. Pools where feeder streams enter can be especially productive in these conditions.

Many fishermen keep daily journals that record water temperatures and benefit greatly from the information. As time goes by, an angler develops a sort of built-in memory log in regard to water temperatures and other conditions that often clicks in automatically when certain situations are encountered.

Nets

Nets are an accessory that can be useful, but not all fishermen like to carry them. They can be a nuisance, particularly in tight conditions on small streams. On the other hand, they can be very important when playing a large trout, and this almost always occurs when one is on big water with plenty of elbow room. Probably the best way to reach a decision is to judge the pros and cons according to the kind of situation you'll be in.

The traditional net has a wooden frame and a mesh bag and is available in several sizes. These are still standard gear for many anglers, but increasingly popular are the stretch-and-release nets with shallow mesh bags made of soft nylon cord to prevent injury or damage to the fish. Collapsible nets that can be attached to a D-ring or belt or stowed in the back pocket of a vest are practical, too, since they don't get in the way.

Another thing to think about before purchasing a net is its weight and how you plan to attach it. Some nets are worn across the back on an elastic cord, and anybody who has used one is aware this can cause a problem. Often the net snags on a limb or other obstacle without the fisherman being aware. The cord stretches, and when the net comes loose it hurtles forward and catches the angler right in the ribs. More practical are the zingers, clips, or magnetic net holders that prevent fumbling with connections, and vests with large pockets in the back in which to stow either rigid-frame or collapsible nets.

Creels

Creels are optional; while they were once considered an integral part of every fly fisherman's equipment, they're not often seen on park streams anymore. The principal reason is the increasing number of anglers who practice catch-and-release. Those who do carry creels generally prefer the soft-side types that are more comfortable to wear than the traditional wicker basket type and which sometimes have insulation to aid in keeping the contents cool. On the other hand, a wicker creel can do double duty as a lunch basket.

Staffs

A wading staff can be useful in a number of ways, particularly in big water when getting from one point to another often looks a lot easier than it really is. At such times a staff can be used to probe the bottom ahead and provide solid support against the forces of the current. Too, it can be used as a hiking staff, as an "extra arm" to assist a fellow angler who gets in over his depth, and as a help in dislodging snagged flies. If a one-piece staff is considered cumbersome, try a sturdy folding model that fits in a holster worn on the belt.

Having balanced tackle, particularly regarding the rod and line, is essential to obtaining the best performance.

SAFETY TIPS

Fishermen face more hazards in the Smokies than those following most other recreational pursuits, particularly when traveling away from the main roads and on the high-elevation waters. For example, there's a big difference in hiking the trails and in following the stream beds because most small streams drop sharply off the mountainsides and follow twisting, narrow courses that are sometimes strewn with boulders as big as a house. In navigating them there is a constant threat of falls, the result of which may mean broken bones or total disability. This is why it is vital, especially when fishing alone, to advise someone of where you'll be and approximately when you plan to be back.

Provisions

When hiking into remote areas, one should take along plenty of food and water and a change of clothes. All that's needed for a one-day trip can be carried in a small day pack or fanny pack that can be stashed when the destination is reached and returned to at lunchtime and when departing. Having a canteen, bottled water, or a way of treating water suitably is essential since all springs and streams in the Smokies are contaminated and unfit to drink. The problem is caused by the wild boars that invaded the park from adjacent areas many years ago and became well established. These animals wallow in moist places in or near waterways, and their fecal matter contains the eggs and larvae of internal parasites that are highly dangerous to humans. Water purification tablets aren't adequate to eliminate them, although water purification units that filter Giardia are suitable. Some are compact and no heavier than a quart water bottle. They are expensive but worth the price.

44   Storms

Weather is another factor that should be closely observed because it can be exceptionally quixotic in the mountains. In the spring and fall months it's not uncommon for temperatures to plummet from moderate to frigid in a very short time. Snow quite often accompanies these sudden thermometer plunges. In these periods it's worthwhile to have a sweater, fishing vest with zip-on sleeves, or other warm outer garment just in case. In the summer sudden cloudbursts may occur that can transform a small stream into a raging torrent in a matter of minutes, sweeping away anything in its path. This is most likely to occur in narrow valleys bordered by watersheds with steep slopes. In this situation an enormous amount of rainwater is rapidly flushed down the hillsides and into the stream. Some well-known waters are particularly prone to this: Ramsay Prong, the Left Fork of Deep Creek, West Prong of the Little Pigeon, and Bradley Fork, to name a few. If caught in such a downpour, for safety's sake get out of the water and climb to a spot well above the stream bed, and stay there until well after the storm has ceased.

The best precaution is to check the latest forecast before going afield. Regardless of season, sudden rains are common in the mountains. Most veteran Smokies anglers usually have a light rain jacket along in the cooler months when getting soaked can be a very uncomfortable experience.

Sunburn

Much is known now about the detrimental effects of too much sun, so wearing long-sleeved shirts and broad-brimmed hats is sensible. The use of sunblock is also recommended. Stream cover may seem to make this precaution unnecessary, but there's usually more sunlight filtering through than is realized.

Insects

About the only problem insects are tiny and annoying "no-see-um" gnats prevalent in the early morning and late afternoon hours during the summer months, and wasps and hornets that build nests on overhanging limbs fishermen can inadvertently bump into. Repellent can ward off the gnats, and, if bitten, Benadryl is effective in reducing itching. The threat from hornets and wasps exists mainly on the streams since their nests overhang the water, and anglers should keep a keen eye out for them while wading. On the other hand, yellow jackets build their nests underground, and stepping on the entrance can create havoc. The stings of these insects can be dangerous, even fatal, and persons who have a medical history of violent reactions from stings should include the medication necessary to counteract the toxic effects in their first-aid kits. Another useful item to have along is the small, pocket-size kit, available from places like The Sawyer Company, that contains a suction device to remove poison from insect, spider, and snake bites.

It is interesting to note that insect bites and stings are the number one reported accidents annually in the park.

Snakes

As for snakes, pit vipers such as copperheads and rattlesnakes inhabit much of the park, but they actually pose a minimal threat to anglers. Pit vipers go streamside only during periods of very dry weather since they don't like the noises of running water. These snakes normally derive all of the moisture they require from the rain that collects in various parts of the forest floor. Normally pit vipers inhabit deadfalls and rocky areas. The best rule is to not put your hands where they don't

46 belong. Simply pay attention to where you are and what you're doing, especially when navigating from trail to stream.

Nonpoisonous water snakes are fairly common in lower-elevation streams, but at higher altitudes reptiles of any variety are seldom seen. Part of the reason for the relative rarity of snakes in the park is that they're preyed on by both bears and wild boar. The latter animals seek them out zealously.

One last point: Being prepared—equipment, clothing, provisions, safety measures, etc.—from the outset will spare the beginner many hours of frustration and make for a good start on Day One on the stream. However, there's still the matter of becoming familiar with park streams. To accomplish this, there's no better way than employing the services of a professional guide. He or she can take you to the kind of water you prefer to fish and familiarize you with the most popular fly patterns.

4

Techniques and Tactics

CASTING THE SMOKIES

FISHING LARGER WATERS WHERE THERE IS PLENTY of room requires using only standard casting procedures that are quite easily learned. However, since much of the fishing in the Smokies is in small streams where tight cover can severely restrict casting room, it is important the angler be familiar with, and hopefully adept at, the techniques necessary for successfully working such waters.

Often the most productive spots are so overgrown with vegetation it is impossible to reach them with the casting methods used on larger streams. Short, very accurate, casts of sometimes little more than a few yards or less in distance are required. This means the fisherman must use some entirely different type casts to achieve success. For instance, one needs to be able to cast backhand as well as forehand, and from all kinds of unusual positions. Those lucky few who are ambidextrous have a distinct advantage in performing some of the necessary motions.

When fishing the small streams, it's important to know how to cast in close quarters. Even then, one can expect hang-ups.

Roll Casting

One of the most valuable techniques is the tight roll cast that eliminates the need for a back cast and which can be accomplished with the rod in either a vertical or horizontal position. What will help make this cast more effective is to use a leader with a heavy butt section of about three feet in length, tapered down from that point to whatever tippet strength is desired. This makes the fly turn over more easily and is beneficial in other short casting methods, as well.

Bow-and-Arrow Casting

Another close-quarters favorite is the bow-and-arrow cast, accomplished by gripping the fly by the bend of the hook and bending the rod back until it makes a bow. When released, the fly shoots out like an arrow. This is a cast that works when all others fail, and it can be delivered from a standing or kneeling position.

Creative Casting

Sometimes it's possible to find a hole in the vegetation into which a cast can be directed, but this requires precision and an unusual procedure. Facing the hole rather than the stream, make a forward cast into the opening, then slowly pivot and make another forward cast to place the fly. Using a backhand cast to put the fly into the hole and following through with a regular forward cast can accomplish the same thing. Experienced anglers can also snap the line up into holes straight above, then redirect the cast forward as the line descends.

If there is a little room between the overhead obstacles and the water, casting horizontally from a kneeling position to work the line in the available space can make it possible to put a fly into a hard-to-reach spot.

Slack-Line Casting

As for the downstream presentation of dry flies, nymphs, and streamers when a true cast isn't possible, the slack-line technique is very useful. This is accomplished by dropping the fly into the water and feeding out line rapidly so it doesn't drag. The rod tip can assist in determining the direction of line drift in the current, and this approach can often allow otherwise inaccessible spots to be fished very effectively.

Versatility is the name of the game on small streams, and fishermen who practice various casting methods and become accomplished will increase their chances of success significantly. After all, it is logical that the places most difficult to reach will be those the biggest trout prefer to inhabit.

TACTICS

Stealth is a term extremely important to successful fly fishing, and there are a number of factors to which it refers. All anglers are aware that trout are very sensitive to sounds or vibrations and that their vision is uncannily sharp. Because of these characteristics, there are certain basic rules that must be constantly kept in mind and followed as closely as possible.

- Wear neutral-colored clothing, such as khaki, or patterned fabrics that blend with the environment. Trout can spot bright colors from a distance, so regardless of how attractive these kinds of garments may seem to the angler, they can be poison on the stream.

- Approach each spot you plan to fish slowly and quietly. Quick movements spook trout, and splashing or stumbling over rocks sends out sound waves that have the same effect.

- Try to approach the places you have targeted to fish with the sun or available light at your back. The eyes of trout cannot adjust to light conditions, and they are virtually blind when facing the sun.

- If you snag a fly over a prospective location, break it off and tie on a new one rather than disturb the spot and lose a chance to pick up a fish. Once you've finished fishing the spot, you can try to retrieve it with no harm done.

- When practical, it is wise to leave the water and carefully scout a particularly appealing pool or stretch of water from a distance in order to determine the best way to approach and fish it. There may be avenues of opportunity that can't be seen from one angle.

- If you miss a nice fish in a pool, leave it alone and keep moving on. Try it again later in the day when you are coming back downstream or on your way out.

- Stop frequently and look ahead for any surface activity. Sometimes trout are feeding actively on some food source such as ants or inchworms.

- On small streams in particular, it's important to keep a very low profile as you move along. The water is likely to be gin-clear and shallow, permitting the trout to see everything that moves.

- When possible, try to keep false casts to a minimum in order to keep the line moving overhead from spooking the trout. This is where an angler proficient with the roll cast has a big advantage.

■　At places where very little cover exists, do not hesitate to crawl into casting position on your hands and knees because it is the only approach that is likely to pay off. This applies particularly to slow, flat runs with grassy banks where your profile would spook trout many yards away.

READING WATER

Veteran anglers know the art of reading, or analyzing, water, which is the ability to determine the places in a stream where trout are most likely to be positioned. This skill is highly important to successful fly fishing.

This is a talent not easily achieved. It takes a lot of observation and experimentation, which equates to time on the water. You may spend hours studying the currents and surface activity before attempting to fish. However, it is time well spent because the learning process can be interesting, exciting, and rewarding. Once understood and in practice, it will be a source of unending pleasure. Every stream has an individual personality, so there are different challenges at each new location.

One of the advantages of being able to read water is that it makes an angler aware that virtually every part of a stream has potential, even if it may appear to be barren of fish. Many anglers fish only those places that look good, particularly pools that provide easy access. They hopscotch up a stream searching them out, leaving the water between alone. Ironically, they are seldom able to fish even these prime spots efficiently. The most they accomplish is to put the trout down.

There are a number of factors involved in discovering how to read water, all basic and easily understood.

Pools

First, trout usually face into the current for the logical reason that this is where the food comes from, whether on or under the surface. Generally, the water flow is in a downstream direction, but there are exceptions. Pools, for instance, may have backswings where the current is reversed, and there are often eddies and other niches where it is almost undetectable. These are the places where it is easiest to see rising fish.

A pool, particularly a fairly large one, will have a variety of spots in which trout may be holding. Therefore, pools are usually the most complex kind of water to decipher. An example would be a pool with fast white water at its head, one or more large rocks either above or below the surface that divert part of the current into a backwater, a shallow gravel bar along one side, and a smooth, shallow tailwater up which the fisherman must wade to get into position to cast.

Visually studying the location may indicate each of the spots has potential, but that's only half of the solution. Accompanying the business of reading water is having the knowledge of how to fish it. In the case of the theoretical example just presented, an angler using the right approach may be able to touch all of the bases, beginning at the terminal end and working forward.

Shallows

As mentioned, pools are the places that ordinarily get the most pressure and as a result can be the hardest to fish. There are other types of water fishermen must learn. In fact, the art of reading water isn't complete until all of them have been examined and figured out.

Fishing the hard-to-reach spots on the small streams is often where the best action is.

What assists most is understanding how little water is required to hold and hide trout and that very shallow areas are often the places of the most activity. Brown trout roam everywhere when feeding and will charge into spots barely deep enough to cover their dorsal fins. Riffles are a good example of this because often they're little over ankle-deep and overlooked and unmolested by the majority of fishermen. It's a mistake to do so because many contain little pockets of water that carry fish. No doubt some don't offer much promise, but others may provide enough action to keep an angler busy for awhile and places to remember for the next trip.

Deeps

Fast, deep water should not be bypassed either since there are usually quiet places close to shore where trout feed. Also, small dark spots in the tumbling water indicate underwater rocks, and putting a dry fly over them may raise trout lurking behind. These runs are favorites of anglers using weighted nymphs, which can get down to where the trout hold when there's no surface activity.

Those Out-of-the-Way Places

Many places that produce the best fish have to be carefully sought out since they are often unobtrusive and ignored by most fishermen. Quite frequently they are the places that seem invulnerable, such as small pockets guarded by branches that overhang or even dip into the water. Undercut banks are favorite trout haunts, as well as places where water flows through root masses or sweeps under logs or other obstacles in the stream. Experienced anglers can usually read these kinds of waters and come up with a solution to putting a fly into them,

56 and sometimes, when trout are sulking, these tough-to-get-at spots are the last resort for a payoff.

READING FEEDING ACTIVITY

Something that goes hand-in-hand with learning to read water is being able to understand what kind of feeding activity, if any, may be taking place. Knowing how to correctly identify feeding patterns will help shape your decision on what to use and how to present it.

Obviously, prominent hatches pose no problem beyond trying to determine what is coming off and what size it is. But tailing or bulging may suggest trout are feeding just under the surface, which means emerging nymphs or some other form of food gliding along in the current. Likewise, fast and furious surface activity generally suggests a lot of smaller trout are on the prowl—although this can be deceptive. Unlike big rainbows, which tend to remain deep and prey on minnows and crawfish, brown trout never get so large they won't go after tiny insects, and they can pluck a fly off the surface so delicately only a dimple remains. Many anglers have tied into monster browns while casting to what they believed to be ten- to twelve-inch rainbows.

Fishing weighted nymphs can often be highly productive since by using them, an angler can probe the deeper pools and runs where trout are holding close to the bottom. Also, sometimes trout can be coaxed into striking by using large, gaudy flies that don't represent any particular kind of insect; cast over the pool several times with the oddball fly, then switch back to a standard pattern.

Finally, at those times when no hatches are occurring and nymphs, wet flies, and streamers won't pay off, using both red and black ant imitations can save the day.

Learning and utilizing the techniques and tactics described here are certain to make your trips more enjoyable and successful. Basically, the whole idea is to outwit trout, and that part is up to you!

Selecting the proper fly is always a challenge, but there are some favorites that pay off well in park waters.

5

Flies

OF ALL THE BASIC COMPONENTS, FLIES ARE THE most important because these imitations of insect and other food forms lie at the very heart of the sport. The challenge of deceiving trout with artificial lures is one that is never fully achieved or satisfied—and happily so, even though an incurable addiction may be created in the process of trying.

Fly fishing has traditionally been viewed as a sport shrouded in mystery and intrigue, a kind of black magic too complex for a layman to understand, much less attempt to master. Flies play a prominent role in this misconception since the language of fly fishermen involves not only colorful and romantic names such as Parmachene Belle, Wickham's Fancy and Royal Coachman, but also puzzling Latin terms like *Diptera, Ephemeroptera,* and *Plecoptera.*

This misconception is rapidly disappearing. Fly fishing is one of the fastest-growing sports in America, and where it was once predominantly male territory, its ranks include an increasing number of women and children.

If there's any mystery remaining, it may lie in the matter of choosing the fly that not only matches the hatch in appearance, but also in size, and because of this flies are tied on a wide range of hook types and sizes that may be as large as #2 or as

Analyzing feeding activity correctly can be the key to success, and often one hook size or one color variation can make the difference.

tiny as #22. The references in the chart that will soon follow indicate the preferred sizes for matching hatches.

The streams in the Smokies have long been favorites of fly fishermen from all over the eastern part of the nation, and some are truly legendary. Hazel Creek, Cataloochee, Little River, and Deep Creek are names recognized by virtually every follower of the sport. Undoubtedly, these and lesser known streams of the Smokies represent one of the best wild fisheries in the nation.

Many fly-fishing greats have fished these waters, but it is doubtful any have ever approached the remarkable skill of Mark Cathey, who fished the Smokies' streams for more than fifty years from the late 1890s until the 1940s. Cathey, a native of the Deep Creek section near Bryson City, North Carolina, was a magician with a dry fly, using a unique tactic that was awe-inspiring and deadly. In his long-out-of-print book *Hunting and Fishing in the Great Smokies,* Jim Gasque detailed this presentation, which involved delicately dancing a dry fly back and forth on the water to simulate an insect struggling to get off the surface. The fly was never more than twenty feet away, sometimes much closer, and he retrieved it only when a fish was on.

According to Gasque, "He and his rod were like one smooth-working machine, with the greater life coming from the bobbing fly instead of the machine that gave it life."

Gasque also describes a method, almost directly opposite this approach, used by two local men to catch big rainbow trout on Cataloochee Creek. It was unorthodox, to say the least, but extremely effective.

The rig consisted of a large fly, #4 or #6 attached to a #2 or #3 Colorado or Idaho spinner. Small lead shot were strung about a foot apart the full length of the leader with the tail shot far enough away from the spinner to not detract from its action. With this they could fish the larger pools right down to the bottom. None of the niceties of fly fishing were employed.

In addition to Gasque's book, there are several others that chronicle trout fishing adventures during the early part of the century: *Twenty Years Hunting and Fishing in the Great Smoky Mountains* by Sam Hunnicut and *Papa Was a Fisherman* by Joe Long.

In the early years many anglers preferred to use wet flies, fishing crosswise or downstream, sometimes using two or three flies. The shift in interest to dry flies came about mainly due to the development of better equipment. Today's floating fly lines, for instance, are a far cry from the old braided silk lines that had to be dressed frequently to prevent waterlogging. Too, tapered, knotless, monofilament leaders are vastly superior to the old gut leaders that had to be soaked overnight prior to a trip to make them lie flat on the water. Important also are the lighter, tougher, more responsive rods that are easier to handle.

This doesn't mean wet flies aren't important; under certain conditions such as high or murky water, they are still very effective. A good way to fish both wet and dry flies simultaneously is to use a dropper loop in the leader—a technique particularly favored by nymph fishermen. A typical example would be a big, high-floating Wulff fly tied off the dropper loop and a nymph on the terminal end of the leader. This way the dry fly serves as an indicator of what is happening to the nymph and can detect strikes that would otherwise be undetected. Another method just as effective and currently very popular is the use of strike indicators made of puttylike substances, yarn, or buoyant tape.

SMOKIES HATCHES

The Smokies park has a wide variety of aquatic and terrestrial insects, and fly fishermen from other parts of the nation can expect to find most of the species common in their home waters. What they won't experience are the periodic or occasional massive hatches of aquatic insects they may be accustomed to seeing in other places.

Acidic Water Conditions

Smokies streams have adequate hatches, yet not spectacular ones, because the water in all but one of the Smokies watersheds is infertile and slightly acidic, factors that inhibit aquatic insect growth and reproduction. In terms of aquatic insects, however, the park streams are some of the most diverse in North America, and over the past several years entomologists have discovered more than twenty new species.

As mentioned earlier, this acidic condition is caused by the geology of the mountains, or more specifically, one of its major structures. Most of the crest of the Smokies are underlain by the Thunderhead and Anakeesta formations. The Thunderhead formation is sandstone, which weathers slowly and adds nothing to enhance stream quality. The most prominent example of this formation can be seen at the parking area at Clingman's Dome. Anakeesta formation is made up of metamorphic rocks such as slate and phyllite; some of its better-known exposures are Charlies Bunion and the Sawteeth on the Appalachian Trail, the crest of the Chimney Tops, and Alum Cave Bluffs.

The Anakeesta formation contains the mineral pyrite, which is an iron ore. Sulfuric acid is produced by oxidation as normal weathering breaks down the pyrite. This often leaves a

Employing the services of a professional guide who is familiar with stream conditions and hatching schedules can be of great benefit to anglers unfamiliar with the park streams.

telltale rusty iron stain on the rocks. The big area of exposed rock at Newfound Gap parking area is a good example, and there are several others where landslides and road construction have taken place (any fresh exposure releases more than the usual amount of sulfuric acid).

Because of the extent of the Anakeesta formation and its many outcrops, virtually all of the streams in the Smokies are affected. The exception is the Abrams Creek watershed, which is underlain by limestone and free of acidic influence. Understandably, this is where the most prolific aquatic insect hatches in the park occur.

Hatch Schedules

The radical altitude variations in the Smokies create different climate zones, which makes it impossible to develop an insect hatch chart or schedule of consistent uniformity. However, there is a guide available that goes a long way in helping solve the puzzles: *A Smoky Mountains & Southern Appalachians Fly Hatch Schedule* (Graphic Spirit, 1991), produced by Ken Snelling with assistance from Carl Rogers and critical acknowledgment by David Etnier, a Ph.D. and professor of zoology at the University of Tennessee.

It has already been mentioned that there may be brookies feeding on nymphs very early in the year in high-altitude streams. However, what isn't as well known among fishermen unfamiliar with park waters is that there is also both nymph and dry fly opportunity during the winter months at the lower altitudes. Midge, stonefly, and caddis fly hatches occur throughout December, January, and February in waters below about two thousand feet. These are tiny winter insects that require 16- to 22-size flies, as well as a sharp eye to detect their presence.

Dry fly fishing is at its best in April, May, and June, with a wide variety of stonefly, caddis fly, Mayfly, and midge activity from early morning through late afternoons. It's a period during which many of the larger forms are hatching, and 8- to 10-size dry flies and 2- to 6-size nymphs can be especially effective. At most other times of the year, much smaller dry fly sizes are required, the average being in the 12- to 14-size; but in some patterns 18- to 22-size dry flies are needed. The same applies to nymphs, but in streamers, which usually simulate minnow forms, the larger hook sizes are almost always suitable.

From June to August the trout diet is heavily supplemented by a diversity of terrestrials such as grasshoppers, crickets, bees, wasps, ants, beetles, caterpillars, and jassids. Abundant stonefly, caddis fly, mayfly, and midge hatches are also occurring, so there's an extremely wide choice of offerings that are likely to pay off.

Hook size is as important as the pattern in matching a hatch. Trout will ignore a fly that may appear identical but which is either larger or smaller than the insects upon which they are feeding.

Terrestrials are still favored fly patterns until about the end of September, but during that month and on through October and November several kinds of caddis and midge hatches continue to occur.

Put simply, the park streams offer year-round activity for the fly fisherman who is willing to endure whatever weather conditions exist. And since there's no closed season on any of the waters where fishing is allowed, all it takes is the desire to do it. It's vital to recognize that hook size is as important as the pattern in matching a hatch. A trout will ignore a fly that may appear identical to, but that is either larger or smaller than, the insects upon which they are feeding.

FLY PATTERNS 67

There is an untold number of fly patterns that could be recommended for Smokies streams, but naming them all would be burdensome. (Please see Appendix B: Fly Hatch and Pattern Chart for a more comprehensive list.) It will be more helpful to list some traditional favorites, many or most of which will be found in every veteran park fisherman's collection. Beyond this selection are many other kinds of nymphs and terrestrials such as beetles, ants, and jassids that could also be added to fly boxes.

Some of the flies included in the illustrations following this list had their origin in the Smokies, invented and tied by local fishermen or by those from nearby who fished the streams regularly. Principal among these are the Tellico nymph, Thunderhead, Yellow Hammer (both dry and nymph versions), Sheep Fly, and several Adams variants.

Dry Flies

(1) Adams, (2) Parachute Adams, (3) Thunderhead, (4) Yellow Hammer, (5) Light Cahill, (6) Blue-Dun Thorax, (7) Green Humpy, (8) Yellow Humpy, (9) Bullet-Head Grasshopper, (10) Royal Wulff, (11) Carolina Wulff, (12) Tennessee Wulff, (13) Orange Palmer, (14) Yellow Palmer, (15) Black Elk-Hair Caddis, (16) Chartreuse Elk-Hair Caddis, (17) Female Olive Caddis

Nymphs

(1) Sheep Fly, (2) Secret Weapon, (3) Tellico, (4) Peacock Wooly Worm, (5) My Pet, (6) Pheasant Tail, (7) Prince, (8) Hare's Ear, (9) C. K. Nymph, (10) Yellow Stonefly Creeper, (11) Chartreuse Inchworm

68 Streamers

(1) Muddler Minnow, (2) Woolly Bugger, (3) Yellow Hammer, (4) Black Ghost, (5) Gray Ghost, (6) Mickey Finn

THE "RECIPES"*

Following are instructions for tying each of the patterns. (For illustrations of these flies, please see plate #1 in the color insert.)

Dry Flies

(1) *Adams:* Tail—brown and grizzly hackle fibers or moose hair; body—muskrat; wings—grizzly hackle tips; hackle—brown and grizzly mixed. Hook—Mustad 94840 or equivalent, sizes 10 to 18. Best March to October.

(2) *Parachute Adams:* Tail—brown and grizzly hackle fibers or moose hair; body—muskrat; wings—white calf body hair; hackle—brown and grizzly mixed. Hook—Mustad 94840 or equivalent, sizes 12 to 20. Good year around.

(3) *Thunderhead:* Tail—moose or deer hair; body—muskrat; wings—white calf body hair; hackle—brown. Hook—Mustad 94840 or equivalent, sizes 10 to 16. Best March to September.

(4) *Yellow Hammer:* Tail—ginger hackle fiber; body—yellow floss; rib—guinea feather dyed yellow, tied palmer, and clipped; wings—wood duck flank feather; hackle—ginger. Hook—Mustad 94840 or equivalent, sizes 10 to 16. Best April to August.

(5) *Light Cahill:* Tail—light ginger or cream hackle fibers; body—bleached opossum or cream fur; wings—wood duck flank; hackle—light ginger or cream. Hook—Mustad 94840 or equivalent, sizes 12 to 14. Best April to August.

(6) *Blue-Dun Thorax:* Tail—medium dun hackle fibers; body—muskrat; wings—medium dun turkey flats; hackle—medium dun clipped underneath. Hook—Mustad 94840 or equivalent, sizes 12 to 20. Good year around.

(7-8) *Humpy—Green and Yellow:* Tail—deer or elk hair; body—green or yellow floss; wings—deer or elk hair tied in at tail, then pulled over body, tied down at head, and parted; hackle—grizzly brown or grizzly. Hook—Mustad 94840 or equivalent, sizes 10 to 14. Best March to September.

(9) *Bullet-Head Grasshopper:* Body—yellow deer hair; wings—turkey quill; legs—turkey or goose biots; head—deer or elk hair tied in at hook eye, pulled back and tied down, and trimmed underneath. Hook—Mustad 94831, sizes 10 to 16. Good April to October.

(10-11-12) *Wulffs—Royal, Carolina, and Tennessee:* Tail—deer or moose hair; body—peacock herl; color band—red thread for Royal, chartreuse for Tennessee, yellow for Carolina (floss optional); wings—white calf body hair; hackle—dark brown. Hook—Mustad 94840 or equivalent, sizes 10 to 14. Best March to September.

(13-14) *Palmers—Orange and Yellow:* Tail—grizzly hackle fibers; body—range or yellow fur; hackle—grizzly. Hook—Mustad 94840 or equivalent, sizes 12 to 16. Best April to August.

(15-16) *Elk-Hair Caddis—Black, and Chartreuse:* Body—black or chartreuse fur; hackle—brown for Black, light dun for Chartreuse; wings—light elk hair. Hook—Mustad 94840 or equivalent, sizes 12 to 18. Good year around.

(17) *Female Olive Caddis:* Body—olive fur; egg sac—yellow fur; hackle—brown or grizzly; wings—light elk hair. Hook—Mustad 94840 or equivalent, sizes 12 to 18. Good year around.

Some species of caddis flies hatch year around in the park. Here a caddis grub emerges from its protective case beside an artificial caddis grub.

Nymphs

(1) *Sheep Fly:* Tail—brown hackle fibers; body—muskrat; wings—grizzly hackle tips; hackle—brown hen. Hook—Mustad 9671 or equivalent, sizes 6 to 14. Good year around.

(2) *Secret Weapon:* Tail—golden pheasant tippets; body—peacock herl; hackle—brown hen. Hook—Mustad 9671 or equivalent, sizes 10 to 14. Good year around.

(3) *Tellico:* Tail—guinea hackle fibers; wing case—turkey quill; body—yellow floss; rib—peacock herl; hackle—brown hen. Hook—Mustad 9671 or equivalent, sizes 8 to 16. Best March to August.

(4) *Peacock Wooly Worm:* Tail—red hackle feathers (optional); body—peacock herl; hackle—brown, palmered. Hook—Mustad 9671 or equivalent, sizes 10 to 14. Good year around.

(5) *My Pet:* Tail—brown hackle; wing case—turkey quill; body—muskrat; hackle—brown and grizzly. Hook—Mustad 9671 or equivalent, sizes 10 to 14. Good year around.

(6) *Pheasant Tail:* Tail—pheasant tail fibers; abdomen—pheasant tail feathers wound around hook; wing case—pheasant tail fibers; thorax—peacock herl; legs—pheasant tail split by wing case. Hook—Mustad 9671 or equivalent, sizes 12 to 18. Good year around.

(7) *Prince:* Tail—two brown goose biots; body—peacock herl; rib—gold tinsel; hackle—brown hen; wings—two white goose biots. Hook—Mustad 9671 or equivalent, sizes 8 to 14. Good year around.

(8) *Hare's Ear:* Tail—deer hair; abdomen—hare's ear; wing case—pheasant tail; thorax—hare's ear, picked out. Hook—Mustad 9671 or equivalent, sizes 12 to 18. Best March to August.

72

(9) *C. K. Nymph:* Tail—wood duck flank fibers; body—black wool; hackle—grizzly, trimmed and palmered. Hook—Mustad 9671 or equivalent, sizes 10 to 14. Good year around.

(10) *Stonefly Creeper:* Tail—wood duck flank fibers; wing case—wood duck flank fibers; abdomen—stripped ginger hackle stem; thorax—yellow rabbit fur; legs—wood duck flank fibers split by wing case. Hook—Mustad 9671 or equivalent, sizes 8 to 18. Best May to August.

(11) *Chartreuse Inchworm:* Body—chartreuse chenille. Hook—Mustad 9671 or equivalent, sizes 10 to 12. Best June to September.

Streamers

(1) *Muddler Minnow:* Tail—deer hair or turkey quill; body—flat gold tinsel; wing—quirrel tail under turkey quill; head—spun deer hair clipped to shape. Hook—Mustad 79580 or equivalent, sizes 4 to 12. Good year around.

(2) *Woolly Bugger:* Tail—black marabou; body—dark olive chenille; hackle—grizzly, palmered. Hook—Mustad 79580 or equivalent, sizes 4 to 12. Good year around.

(3) *Yellow Hammer:* Tail—dyed yellow quail wing feather fibers; body—peacock herl; rib—copper wire; hackle—yellow-dyed quail wing, palmered. Hook—Mustad 79580 or equivalent, sizes 10 to 14. Best April to August.

(4) *Black Ghost:* Tail—yellow hackle fibers; body—black wool or floss; rib—flat silver tinsel; throat—yellow hackle fibers; cheeks—jungle cock eyes. Hook—Mustad 79580 or equivalent, sizes 4 to 12. Good year around.

(5) *Gray Ghost:* Tail—none; body—orange wool or floss; rib—flat silver tinsel; throat—white calf tail under golden pheasant crest; wing—peacock herl under golden pheasant

crest under four dun hen hackles. Hook—Mustad 79580 or   **73**
equivalent, sizes 4 to 12. Good year around.

(6) *Mickey Finn:* Tail—none; body—flat silver tinsel; wing—yellow buck tail under red buck tail under yellow buck tail. Hook—Mustad 79580 or equivalent, sizes 4 to 12. Good year around.

*Fly illustrations and fly-tying instructions courtesy of Derek Porter, Brevard, North Carolina.

There are several large streams in the Pigeon River drainage that offer fly fishermen—and fisherwomen—plenty of elbow room.

6

The Smokies Map and Additional Information

NGLERS PLANNING TO FISH PARK STREAMS HAVE
the choice of staying in nearby towns that offer restaurants, motels, and hotels. However, for those who like to
camp, whether it be at sites with facilities for recreational vehicles and trailers or in primitive sites in the backcountry, there's
an enormous amount of opportunity within the park.

The more modern campgrounds are ideal for family
groups and can serve as convenient headquarters from which
to operate and roam by car or on foot in various parts of
the park. For the avid fisherman, it is the backcountry location
that affords the greatest opportunity to fish the remote, high-
elevation streams that get minimal pressure. There is something special in having a private haven far removed from the
mainstream of activity.

As *The Great Smoky Mountains Trail Map* and the *Backcountry Campsites and Shelters* chart in the back of the book indicates, there are many types of campsites. By carefully examin-
ing the list it will be easy for the fisherman to identify those that
offer the best possibilities for privacy in the vicinity of trout
water. Also reprinted is information on the backcountry camp-

Signs like this that explain the fishing regulations are posted throughout the park.

sites, permits, and rules and regulations that apply. The map is   *77*
available free and distributed at all park visitor centers.

USING THE CHART

Backcountry campsites and shelters are listed by map coordinates (7E, etc.) with elevations in feet. Backcountry campsites are numbered and grouped by major access areas. All sites and shelters are available to hikers; camping with horses is allowed only at those sites marked with a bold H. Shelters and sites whose use is rationed appear in bold type; their allowable capacities show in parentheses. Therefore "(12, 6H)" denotes a capacity for twelve hikers and six horses while "(12)" means twelve hikers and no horses.

PERMITS—HOW AND WHY

The backcountry permit is free but is required for all overnight camping in the backcountry. If you intend to stay overnight in the backcountry, you will need a permit. The backcountry permit is designed to protect the park and its solitude, both the quality of the natural environment and the quality of your experience. The National Park Service is charged with protecting the Smokies for present and future generations to enjoy. The permit system is an attempt to enable you and others to love this wild place without loving it to death.

HOW TO GET YOUR BACKCOUNTRY PERMIT

You may self-register for a permit at any ranger station by following posted instructions, but your itinerary may require access to a public pay telephone, as explained below.

Some sites are rationed (refer to the chart) because of heavy use. You must telephone the park's Backcountry Reservation Office to obtain permission for the use of one of these sites. Failure to do so invalidates your permit and puts you in violation of regulations and subject to a fine.

If your itinerary includes at least one rationed site, the National Park Service encourages you to make advance reservations up to a month ahead of the trip's start. To do so, you must plan your trip before your call and indicate exactly which site you intend to occupy for each night of your trip. If no rationed sites are involved, you may obtain your permit via self-registration upon your arrival at the park. The Backcountry Reservation Office is open seven days a week, from 8 A.M. to 6 P.M. The telephone number is (423) 436-1231.

The following rules relate to trip planning:

RULES AND REGULATIONS

- You must possess a backcountry permit while camping in the backcountry.
- Camping is permitted only at designated sites and shelters.
- You must stay in designated sites and follow your identified itinerary.
- Use of rationed sites and shelters must be confirmed through the Backcountry Reservation Office.

- You may stay up to three consecutive nights at a site. You may stay no more than one night in a row at a shelter.
- Maximum camping party size is eight persons.
- Open fires are prohibited except at designated camp sites. Use only wood that is dead and on the ground.
- Use of tents at shelters is prohibited.
- Food storage: When not being consumed or transported, all food and trash must be suspended at least ten feet off the ground and four feet from the nearest limb or trunk or stored as otherwise designated.
- Toilet use must be at least one hundred feet from a camp-site or water source and out of sight of a trail. Human feces must be buried in a six-inch-deep hole.
- All trash must be carried out.
- All plants, wildlife, and natural and historic features are protected by law. Do not cut, carve, or deface any trees or shrubs.
- Polluting park waters is prohibited; do not wash dishes or bathe with soap in a stream.
- Pets, motorized vehicles, and bicycles are not permitted in the backcountry.
- Firearms and hunting are prohibited.
- Feeding or harassing any wildlife is prohibited.

Note: The maximum fine for each violation is $500 and/or six months in jail.

In addition, certain courtesies help to make the permit system work for everyone: (1) Do not reserve more space than you intend to occupy; to do so prohibits use by other backpackers. (2) Please call the reservation office to cancel any nights or spaces that become available because of changes in your plans.

The small, high-elevation streams offer prime fishing potential, but they are crystal clear and must be approached stealthily.

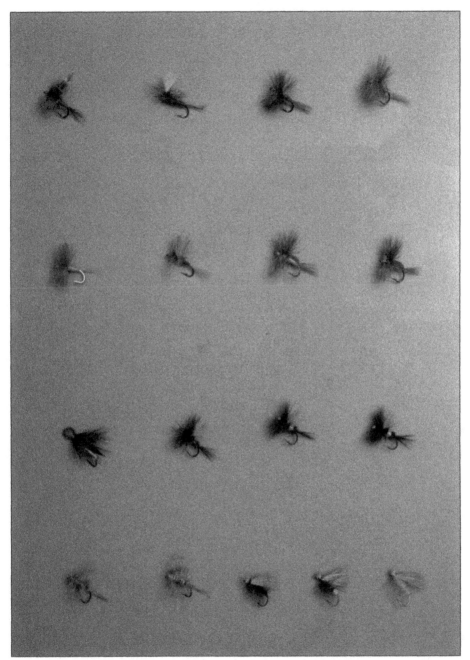

Left to Right: *top row,* Adams, Parachute Adams, Thunderhead, Yellow Hammer; *second row,* Light Cahill, Blue-Dun Thorax, Green Humpy, Yellow Humpy; *third row,* Bullet-Head Grasshopper, Royal Wulff, Carolina Wulff, Tennessee Wulff; *bottom row,* Orange Palmer, Yellow Palmer, Black Elk-Hair Caddis, Chartreuse Elk-Hair Caddis, Female Olive Caddis.

Left to Right: *top row,* Sheep Fly, Secret Weapon, Tellico, Peacock Wooly Worm; *second row,* My Pet, Pheasant Tail, Prince, Hare's Ear; *third row,* C. K. Nymph, Yellow Stonefly Creeper, Chartreuse Inchworm; *fourth row,* Muddler Minnow, Wooly Bugger, Yellow Hammer; *bottom row,* Black Ghost, Gray Ghost, Mickey Finn.

The southern Appalachian brook trout is found in streams at the highest elevations within the park.

Landing a rainbow trout in the Middle Prong of the Little Pigeon River, known within the park as the Greenbriar River.

A selection of streamer flies.

Trophy size rainbow trout frequently are taken from the larger park streams.

An angler preparing to walk into one of the high elevation streams.

Hiking into the brown trout streams provides access to a privacy that is conducive to quiet and solitude.

7

Smokies Streams and Rivers

THERE ARE 333 STREAMS WITHIN THE PARK, AND 2,108 miles of water, more than seven hundred miles of which contain trout. Some hold all species: rainbow, brown, and brook. Others hold rainbow and brook or rainbow and brown, and a few contain only brook trout. They are well distributed throughout the region in what biologists have identified as forty-five different watersheds, although some watersheds whose waters eventually join to create major streams or rivers are linked together and considered as one system. Others are entirely separate and must be treated as single units.

HIGH-ALTITUDE FISHING

The streams in almost all of the watersheds originate near the main crest of the Smokies, often passing through several ecosystems on their tumbling, cascading, and turbulent descent. During their infancy, before enough springs and rivulets combine to produce a larger flow, they are not prime areas for the average fly fishermen since most of the streams at high altitude offer close-quarters conditions that often require some special casting techniques. The late Joe Brooks, fishing editor for *Outdoor Life* magazine and one of the world's leading fly fishing experts, once said that small headwater streams will teach one more about fly fishing than any water he knew. Yet despite these handicaps, trout in these little branches are very cooperative and easy to catch, so anglers can learn the techniques as they go and be successful in the process. Best of all, they provide those anglers who want to get away from it all the best places at which to do it.

A basic rule that applies all through the park is that the higher up you go on a stream, the less competition you will have. Along with this is the fact that the upper waters sometimes hold better-quality trout than are found at lower altitudes. It sounds illogical, but there are reasons. First, some of these streams get very little pressure, so the trout have an opportunity to grow. Second, in periods of very warm weather rising water temperatures cause trout to move into higher-elevation waters to find a comfort zone, and sometimes they do not return. Finally, there are streams that have more abundant food, which enhances trout growth rates.

Unfortunately, these high-altitude waterways also provide the environments most favorable for native Appalachian brook trout survival and reproduction, and for that reason some are off limits to anglers (See the *Restricted Waters* map at the back of this book.). This is not a significant drawback though since there are plenty of other streams "back of beyond" where fishing is legal.

There are two ways to go about fishing the remote waters. If the stream is only a few miles from the nearest place of access, it's possible to make it a one-day adventure: Get an early start and carry a lunch, water, and (just in case) a rain jacket in a small pack. Many fishermen prefer this approach because it allows them to visit a different location every day.

On the other hand, there are many headwater streams too

remote for a one-day trip, and these offer anglers the opportunity to make a two- to three-day backpacking trip and enjoy a special kind of wilderness experience. There are primitive campsites at most of the locations, all of which are shown on the trail map included in this book (See *The Great Smoky Mountains Trail Map* at the back of this book.); some of these backcountry waters receive virtually no fishing pressure throughout the year. Some hold only brook trout, while others have rainbows and browns.

HIRE A GUIDE

For fishermen unfamiliar with the territory, hiring a guide for backpacking trips into remote areas is recommended since they know the best spots and can tailor a trip to the angler's particular needs. Food and transportation is usually included in the package price. It should be noted that only guides licensed by the National Park Service are permitted to take anglers into the backcountry. A current list of the operators can be obtained at the park headquarters.

FINDING THE BEST SPOT FOR YOU

Upper-elevation spots illustrate only one small example of what is available on the park's multifaceted bill of fare. Every drainage or watershed consists of a network of tributaries that join to form the streams best known to anglers. Fly fishermen can choose anything from tiny spring branches that can be hopped across to roaring rivers; from remote, isolated locations that require miles of hiking to reach to waters that are only a few steps from a parked car. There are gentle waters flow-

A pair of fisherman look at a small creek that might also be called a branch, prong, or fork.

ing through meadowlands that can be fished comfortably and casually, riotous waters that charge down mountainsides through boulder-strewn obstacle courses, and waters that provide a variety of conditions throughout their length.

Many of these waterways are significant in size and obviously provide productive fishing water. Others are so tiny they appear hardly worth the effort to fish, but fishermen with curiosity and no reluctance to burrow through tight cover and laurel thickets often find them to be little bonanzas that open up in places with some very productive pools. The same applies to even larger tributaries that may appear uninteresting where a trail crosses, yet which may prove to be quite different in character farther upstream or downstream. In such cases, an urge to do a little exploring can sometimes pay big dividends by revealing special honey-holes not known to other anglers.

Contained within this vast spectrum of stream types are the flow characteristics that require a variety of techniques to fish successfully. It could be argued that rapidly descending streams with plunge pools and very rapid runs are the most challenging. Casting within the runs requires virtual "split-second fishing" where the fly is in the air more often than on the water and high-floating, very visible, dry flies are the best bet. It's a situation where intense alertness and a hair-trigger response is necessary. The plunge pools, on the other hand, are often deep, and in many cases it takes a weighed nymph to get down to where the trout are holding, although if there is a large enough surface area, a dry fly will work just fine.

On slower-moving streams with big pools cut by long flows and riffles, a fisherman has the opportunity to use longer casts and more delicate presentation. In pools the location of feeding fish can be spotted and stalked, and it is usually possible to identify the insect forms on which they are feeding. This is where casting expertise is very important because precise placement of the fly is vital to success.

DEALING WITH PRESSURE

There are many extremely high-profile streams and rivers in the park that invariably attract anglers visiting it for the first time. It's natural this should happen, yet this desire to fish traditionally famous waters often results in pretty crowded conditions.

This does not mean those waters should be ignored, particularly by experienced and skillful fly fishermen who can employ tactics and strategies necessary to lure wary trout. Also, the most pressure on such waters is usually concentrated on the spots most attractive and easily accessible to amateur anglers, leaving plenty of very productive water practically untouched.

If the crowd factor is undesirable, one solution is to select streams considered off the beaten path. This usually means remote waters, but there are also some easily accessible streams that receive minimal pressure simply because many anglers pass them by, assuming they're heavily fished. To cite a few examples: the Little River along which TN Scenic Highway 73 runs for many miles; the West Prong of the Little Pigeon River bordered by US 411 from the park line to more than halfway to Newfound Gap; and on the other side of the mountains, the Oconaluftee River, which is paralleled by US 411 for most of the distance just below Newfound Gap to the park boundary near Cherokee.

THE NAME FACTOR

It should be noted that many tributary streams, large and small, may go by different names according to what map, guide book, or local angler you may be referring to. The terms branch, prong, fork, and creek are sometimes used inter-changeably. For instance, what may be listed as a creek in one reference may appear as a branch in another. Bradley Creek, a tributary of the Oconaluftee River, is often called Bradley Fork. Cataloochee River is also called Cataloochee Creek. On the Little River, Fish Camp Creek is also known as Fish Camp Prong. And on the West Prong of the Little Pigeon River, it's Fighting Creek versus Fittin Creek (which got its name from the many disputes settled along its banks).

DETAILS, DETAILS, DETAILS

In the ensuing chapters, all of the park's major streams and rivers will be covered. Detailed information, including a few suggested flies, will be provided for each, as well as their most important tributaries. Basic facts will also be supplied for the smaller tributaries and feeder streams.

Much can be learned about Smokies streams in the topo-graphic maps mentioned in chapter 2: They are drawn on a large scale and offer a more detailed view of the streams, ter-rain, and trails. For fishermen planning repeated trips to explore and fish various park streams, it would be advanta-geous to obtain a full set of these maps, while those who have a specific stream or watershed in mind need only the quadrangle or quadrangles covering that particular area of the park. The

88   chart below shows which maps are needed for any or all portions of the Smokies park.

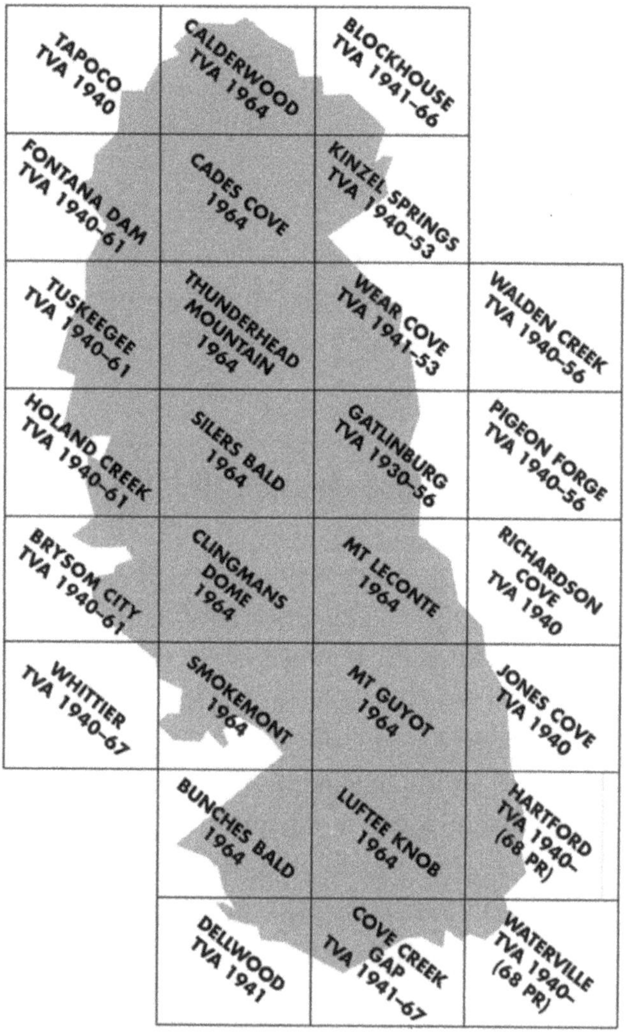

TAPOCO TVA 1940	CALDERWOOD TVA 1964	BLOCKHOUSE TVA 1941-66	
FONTANA DAM TVA 1940-61	CADES COVE 1964	KINZEL SPRINGS TVA 1940-53	
TUSKEEGEE TVA 1940-61	THUNDERHEAD MOUNTAIN 1964	WEAR COVE TVA 1941-53	WALDEN CREEK TVA 1940-56
HOLAND CREEK TVA 1940-61	SILERS BALD 1964	GATLINBURG TVA 1930-56	PIGEON FORGE TVA 1940-56
BRYSOM CITY TVA 1940-61	CLINGMANS DOME 1964	MT LECONTE 1964	RICHARDSON COVE TVA 1940
WHITTIER TVA 1940-67	SMOKEMONT 1964	MT GUYOT 1964	JONES COVE TVA 1940
	BUNCHES BALD 1964	LUFTEE KNOB 1964	HARTFORD TVA 1940- (68 PR)
	DELLWOOD TVA 1941	COVE CREEK TVA GAP 1941-67	WATERVILLE TVA 1940- (68 PR)

GHOSTS OF THE PAST

Along each stream in the Smokies is subtle or obvious evidence of earlier human activity because virtually every waterway, large or small, was at one time inhabited by either single families or a community. Long before the logging operations and other commercial ventures came to the mountains, the pioneers carved out an existence in the most rugged and intimidating territory in the eastern United States. Many built their log cabins miles from any form of civilization, preferring a solitary life in the remote mountain coves and hollows.

What clues remain about these residents of long ago are often very subtle: the ruins of a stone chimney, the crumbling remnants of a rock wall, a patch of daffodils or other exotic flowers, an apple tree, a rusty plowshare, or simply a bare patch of ground, the symmetry of which indicates the location of a cabin or other building long gone.

Some of the trails anglers follow into the backcountry streams were made by these early settlers, either on foot or on ox-drawn sledges used to transport goods for sale or barter on their infrequent trips to the nearest place of commerce. Many other trails are ones originally used by Indians in their travels to hunting grounds or to trade with tribes in other regions.

More visible evidence of previous inhabitants is the old family graveyards that have been preserved by the descendants of the mountain folk since the creation of the park. Access to them is relatively easy in the Tennessee portion of the park, but in North Carolina, where no road follows the boundary for most of its distance along Fontana Lake, they can be reached only on foot or by boat. In an effort to assist local residents in maintaining these cemeteries, an annual "decoration day

There are many places in the park where evidence of earlier activity can be seen. This crumbling structure was a dry kiln for a lumbering operation on Hazel Creek.

is held on which personnel from the National Park Service and local marinas provide a ferry service to take families across the lake to remote cemetery locations.

But by far the most prominent features that speak of earlier activities are the byproducts of the many lumber companies that logged virtually every watershed in the Smokies. The work forces required by some of the big operations were so large that communities were created to accommodate the various needs of both the companies and their employees. Some were small and had facilities like general stores, churches, blacksmith shops, and clinics to serve basic needs. A few, such as the town of Proctor on Hazel Creek with a population of more than two thousand, also had a school, barber shop, pool hall, boarding and club houses, theater, recreation hall, and other amenities.

Most of the major roads and trails along the streams in the park were originally the beds for the logging railroads that penetrated far back into the mountains to haul out the lumber. Some of the trestles remain, now planked over to accommodate park vehicles for emergency purposes.

A colorful and highly detailed history of the logging operations in the Smokies is contained in a recently published book by Ronald G. Schmidt and William S. Hooks titled *Whistle Over the Mountain* (Graphicom Press, 1994). Contained in it are old photographs that illustrate the extent of the environmental damage done by what has been referred to as the "cut-and-run" lumber companies. The remains of some of the structures shown are still standing at a few locations. The places where such artifacts are most prevalent and undisturbed are on the streams on the eastern side of the park that have no road access.

There were also mining operations at several places now within the park. The major ones were copper mines on Hazel

92 Creek and Eagle Creek that produced rich ore but that were shut down either before or after the park was established. In the early years considerable exploration for various other minerals was undertaken, but copper mines were the only ventures that proved to be successful.

Note: Anglers wishing to fish Hazel Creek or Eagle Creek without a long trek on a hiking trail can take advantage of the boat shuttle provided to fishermen by the Fontana Village Marina, (704) 498-2211. The marina also has rental boats. Cable Cove Campground, operated by the U.S. Forest Service, has a launching ramp for those who prefer to use their own boats. There is another USFS facility, Tsali Camp Area, on the Nantahala arm of the lake. Access to Forney Creek and other upper lake streams is best accomplished by operating out of either the Tsali Area or one of the several boat docks in the vicinity: Crisp Dock, Almond Dock, Greasy Branch Dock, Panther Creek Dock, Alarka Dock, and Wilderness Resort Marina. A map and additional information on these operations can be obtained from: Tennessee Valley Authority, Map Division, P.O. Box 1449, Chattanooga, TN 37401, (423) 632-6082.

8

Little River Drainage

EAST PRONG OF LITTLE RIVER

Location: Northwest section

Fishable miles: 22.9

Quads: Wear Cove, Thunderhead Mountain, Gatlinburg

Predominant species: Rainbow and brown trout, with brook trout at higher elevations

Quality: Very good. Excellent fall fishery.

Comments: Fishing is very good along the entire length of this river. Hiking into the backcountry tributary streams offers anglers the opportunity to get away from the crowds, although it is not necessary to do so to find excellent fishing. The stretch along TN 73 is most productive in the spring and fall. Favorite spots are at Elkmont in and around the campground during the off season and above Elkmont from Huskey Branch to Fish Camp Prong for fall runs of browns and spring runs of rainbow. Fish Camp Prong offers some of the best dry fly fishing in the park for rainbows. The area of the main river best for big browns is from the Y near the park boundary to Metcalf Bottoms.

Best flies: Small dry flies (Blue-Winged Olive, Black Midge, and Parachute Adams, sizes 18 to 22), nymphs (Hare's Ear, Black Stone, and Pheasant Tail, sizes 14 to 20), and streamers (Woolly

Many waters such as the Little River can be reached by walking only a few yards from a paved road.

Bugger, Muddler Minnow, Grey Ghost, sizes 6 to 10) are productive in the winter and early spring months. One of the reasons streamers are so popular during this period is that as the big fish come out of the winter doldrums, hatches haven't begun, and small fry from the previous fall's spawning often become major prey. In the summer dry flies (Elk-Hair Caddis, Light Cahills, and Thunderhead, sizes 14 to 16), and nymphs (Tellico, My Pet, and Golden Stone, sizes 10 to 14) are good choices. Dry flies also produce well in early fall, although presenting large attractor patterns (Royal and Carolina Wulff, Dark Elk-Hair Caddis, and Adams, sizes 10 to 14), and various terrestrial imitations (Chartreuse Inchworm, Bullet-Head Grasshopper, and Deer-Hair Ant, sizes 10 to 18) can prove to be more productive.

Access: Tennessee Scenic Highway 73 offers 14.5 miles of easy access to the Little River from where it enters the park at Townsend to a junction where it bears to the right and parallels the Elkmont Road. Between the park boundary at Townsend and the Elkmont Road, numerous small streams with fishable waters enter from both sides of the river. Among them are: White Oak Flats Branch (1.1 miles), Little Brier Branch (1.1), Blanket Creek (1.5), Laurel Branch (1.8), and Shields Branch (1.3). The river follows the Elkmont Road to just below the Elkmont Campground, at which the pavement ends at a locked gate where the Little River Trail begins and follows the gravel road upstream for 4.5 miles to the junction of Little River and Fish Camp Prong. From that point there is a maintained trail that follows the river for another 2.7 miles. The major tributaries on the upper end of the river are Jakes Creek, Fish Camp Prong, and Rough Creek. Small streams with fishable water include: Huskey Creek (1.0 mile), Mids Branch (1.0), and Rich Branch (1.4).

Closed: All or parts of Fish Camp Prong, Meigs Post

Prong, Meigs Creek, Little River and Grouse Creek at their common junction, and Fish Camp Prong and Goshen Creek at their common junction are closed to fishing. Refer to the *Restricted Waters* map at the back of the book and the master list in chapter 2.

Jakes Creek
Fishable miles: 3.1
Quad: Gatlinburg
Predominant species: Rainbow trout
Quality of fishing: Good
Access: Jakes Creek empties into the Little River from the right at the Elkmont Campground, and the Jakes Creek Road allows auto access 0.5 mile to a locked gate. From that point the Jakes Creek Trail remains close to the stream. The only significant small tributary is Newt Prong, with 1.4 miles of fishable water.

Fish Camp Prong
Fishable miles: 3.3
Quad: Silers Bald
Predominant species: Rainbow and brook trout
Quality of fishing: Excellent
Access: Fish Camp Prong enters the Little River 2.3 miles up the Little River Trail. The Fish Camp Prong Trail turns right and closely follows the stream, allowing easy access.

Rough Creek

Fishable miles: 2.4

Quads: Silers Bald, Clingmans Dome

Predominant species: Rainbow and brook trout

Quality of fishing: Fair

Access: Rough Creek flows into the Little River from the left 0.5 mile past Fish Camp Prong, but the Rough Creek Trail is 0.2 mile beyond. The trail doesn't always follow the creek closely, and at 2.0 miles upstream it veers sharply off to the right, then swings back left, crosses the stream, and heads straight up the side of Sugarland Mountain.

MIDDLE PRONG OF LITTLE RIVER

Location: Northwest Section

Fishable miles: 10.3

Quads: Wear Cove, Thunderhead Mountain

Predominant species: Rainbow trout

Quality of fishing: Good

Comments: This stream is good to excellent in the fall when big browns are on their spawning run. Some favorite spots are the waters 0.5 mile above and below the Great Smoky Mountain Institute at Tremont.

Best flies: There is a good population of stoneflies and caddis flies in this stream, and imitations of both the adult form (Blue-Winged Olive, Quill Gordon, March Brown, sizes 14 to 20) and immatures (Black Stone, Grey Caddis Pupa, and Pheasant Tail, sizes 18 to 22) are very productive in late winter and early spring. In summer and fall dry flies (Adams, Elk-Hair

Catch-and-release nets are shallow and made of soft nylon cord that reduces the chance of injuring the fish.

Caddis, and Royal Wulff, sizes 14 to 18) are good throughout, with nymphs (Golden Stone, Brown Stone, and Zug Bug, sizes 4 to 12) and terrestrials (Chartreuse Inchworm, Bullet-Head Grasshopper, and Deer-Hair Ant, sizes 10 to 14) productive in the fall. Because of a prevalence of baitfish, sculpin, and dace minnows, streamer patterns (Muddler Minnow, Black Ghost, and Woolly Bugger, sizes 10 to 14) are especially effective in the winter and early spring months.

Access: The Middle Prong enters the Little River at the place just inside the park known as the Townsend Y where the Laurel Creek Road turns right off TN Scenic Highway 73 to Cades Cove. At 0.2 mile along the Laurel Creek Road the Middle Prong veers to the left and is accessible along the Tremont Road, which is paved for 2.6 miles and graveled for another 3.1 miles to a locked gate and a parking circle. The Middle Prong Trail begins at this point and closely follows the stream to its upper limits. The main tributary is Thunderhead Prong.

Closed: It should be noted that all or parts of Sams Creek, Marks Creek, Lynn Camp Prong, Indian Flats Prong, and Spruce Flats Creek are closed to fishing. Refer to the *Restricted Waters* map at the back of the book and the master list in chapter 2.

Thunderhead Prong

Fishable miles: 2.9

Quad: Thunderhead Mountain

Predominant species: Rainbow trout

Quality of fishing: Good

Access: Thunderhead Prong enters the Middle Prong from the right at the beginning of the Middle Prong Trail. The Defeat Ridge Trail follows the stream for 2.3 miles.

WEST PRONG OF LITTLE RIVER

Location: Northwest Section

Fishable miles: 7.0

Quads: Wear Cove

Predominant species: Rainbow trout

Quality of fishing: Excellent

Comments: While the access along Laurel Creek Road offers good fishing, the best fishing in this stream lies in the backcountry accessible only by hiking the Bote Mountain Trail. A walk of approximately 1.5 miles will deliver you to some top quality water. Upstream from this point is some great pocket water with intermittent riffles and runs. While at places the stream is very small, it has a dense population of wild rainbows.

Best flies: Same as those for the Middle Prong, except for the streamer patterns. Green, Black, and Chartreuse Elk-Hair Caddis and Green and Yellow Humpies, sizes 14 to 16, are also very effective during the summer months.

Access: No maintained trail follows the West Prong of the Little River, which flows under the Laurel Creek Road not far past the Tremont Road junction. There is backcountry trail access on the West Prong Trail that begins on the Tremont Road and extends to the Bote Mountain Trail. It crosses the stream 2.0 miles from the road. The main tributary is Laurel Creek. Small streams with fishable water include: Meadow Branch (1.0 mile) and Long Cove Creek (0.7).

Laurel Creek

Fishable miles: 4.1

Quad: Wear Cove

Predominant species: Rainbow trout

Quality of fishing: Fair

Access: Because Laurel Creek runs alongside the Laurel Creek Road to Cades Cove, there is easy access to it for virtually all of its length.

9

Little Pigeon River System

WEST PRONG OF LITTLE PIGEON RIVER

Location: North Central
Fishable miles: 11.1
Quads: Gatlinburg, Clingmans Dome
Predominant species: Rainbow and brook trout
Quality of fishing: Fair to good
Comments: Because of the easy access from the highway, this stream gets a lot of pressure, and the fishing is very seasonal. There is plenty of open water and an abundant population of small rainbows, making it a stream very suitable for beginners. At the lower levels there are also small-mouth bass. Brook trout fishing is good in the tributaries at the higher elevations, particularly above where Road Prong (which is closed) enters, but there are some nice pockets of brookies in the main river. Favorite spots are the portion of the stream in the vicinity of White Oak Flats and upstream from the Chimneys Picnic Area.

Best flies: Caddis flies and stoneflies are the major aquatic species, and various patterns and sizes of these in either nymphs or dry flies (Henryville Special, Black and Yellow Elk-Hair Caddis, and Quill Gordon, sizes 12 to 18; Black Stone, Pheasant Tail, and Hare's Ear, sizes 10 to 18) will produce throughout the year. Streamers (Woolly Bugger, Grey Ghost, and Muddler Minnow, sizes 8 to 12) are productive in the winter and early spring months. Once spring and summer hatches are underway, large attractor patterns (Orange Palmer, Royal Wulff, and Yellow Hammer, sizes 10 to 14) are reliable choices. In late summer and fall, hoppers, ants, and other terrestrials (Green Inchworm, Joe's Hopper, Jungle Cock Jassid, and Deer-Hair Ant, sizes 10 to 22) get results.

Access: US 441 follows the West Prong from the park boundary at Gatlinburg all the way to its headwaters near Newfound Gap. There is no trail adjacent to the stream, but even when it isn't in sight from the highway, several of the park's "Quiet Walkways" provide easy access. The main tributaries are Roaring Fork, LeConte Creek, and Dudley Creek. Small streams with fishable waters include: Baskin Creek (1.8 miles), Alum Cave Creek (2.0), Fighting Creek (2.1), Hickory Flats Creek (1.3), Sugarland Creek (1.2), and Two Mile Creek (1.8).

Closed: Road Prong is closed to fishing from its confluence with West Prong. Refer to the *Restricted Waters* map in the back of the book and the master list in chapter 2.

Roaring Fork

Fishable miles: 4.8

Quad: Mt. LeConte

Predominant species: Rainbow trout

Quality of fishing: Very good

Access: Turn left on Airport Road in Gatlinburg and follow for 3.2 miles. At this point the one-way Roaring Fork Motor Nature Trail turns right and Roaring Fork Creek becomes accessible about halfway around the loop. Anglers can reach the creek for the rest of the route, although most prefer to park at the end of the road and fish upstream. Backpackers can reach the upper reaches of Roaring Fork on the Trillium Gap Trail. The only feeder stream with fishable waters is Enloe Creek (1.1 miles).

LeConte Creek

Fishable miles: 4.5

Quads: Gatlinburg, Mt. LeConte

Predominant species: Rainbow trout

Quality of fishing: Fair

Access: From the park boundary, The Roaring Fork Motor Nature Trail follows alongside LeConte Creek for 1.8 miles and allows easy auto access. At Cherokee Orchard, a few hundred yards past where the road becomes one way, the Rainbow Falls Trail begins and follows the creek 2.7 miles to Rainbow Falls.

Dudley Creek

Fishable miles: 3.7

Quad: Mt. LeConte

Predominant species: Rainbow trout

Quality of fishing: Fair

Access: The park portion of Dudley Creek can be reached from TN Scenic Route 73 and US 321 about 3.0 miles east of Gatlinburg, where it runs just inside the park boundary. There is no trail along this portion. The best access is 1.0 mile east where the Twin Creeks trail begins and follows the creek for 2.7 miles to the junction with the Graveyard Ridge Trail. One tributary, Little Dudley Creek, has 1.5 miles of fishable water.

Big, deep pools on the larger waters are places that often hold rainbows and browns of bragging size.

MIDDLE PRONG OF LITTLE PIGEON RIVER

Location: North Central

Fishable Miles: 5.1

Quads: Mt. LeConte, Mt. Guyot

Predominant species: Rainbow trout

Quality of fishing: Fair

Comments: This is another of the rivers that offers very easy access, and as a result it gets a lot of attention. It is also a stream prone to flash floods, which scour the bottom and deplete aquatic insect life. The most productive water is from the ranger station to the picnic area, and one of its main tributaries, Porters Creek, offers good fishing and easy wading.

Best flies: Essentially the same as those for the West Prong, with some excellent hatches of yellow stoneflies in late spring and early summer.

Access: The Middle Prong of the Little Pigeon, also known as Greenbrier, is 5.5 miles from downtown Gatlinburg on US 321 and TN 73. A paved road follows the river for 3.2 miles, where you then turn left onto a gravel road marked as Ramsay Cascades Road for 1.9 miles. There is a parking lot, and from that point the Ramsay Cascades Trail is beside the river for an additional 0.9 mile. The river then turns right, and an unmaintained trail runs beside it to where Buck Fork enters. The major tributaries are Porters Creek, Ramsay Creek, and Webb Creek, although the course of the latter is outside the park, except for its headwater, which begins in the park with 2.4 fishable miles and which is later joined by several other streams originating inside the park: Soak Ash Creek (1.2 miles), Snake Feeder Branch (1.8), Texas Creek (2.4), Timothy Creek (3.0), Ramsay Creek (1.4), Redwine Creek (1.7), and Noisy Creek

(2.3). Copeland Creek (1.9) also begins in the park but joins the river below the boundary. Small streams with fishable water include: Big Bird Branch (0.5 mile), Big Laurel Branch (0.5), Injun Creek (1.5), and Rhododendron Creek (2.0) miles.

Closed: No fishing is permitted on Middle Prong or Buck Fork above where the two meet. Refer to the *Restricted Waters* map at the back of the book and the master list in chapter 2.

Porters Creek

Fishable miles: 5.0

Quad: Mt. LeConte

Predominant species: Rainbow trout

Quality of fishing: Good spring fishery

Access: Porters Creek enters the Middle Prong at the place where it turns left on the Ramsay Cascades gravel road. The paved road follows Porters Creek for 1.0 mile and ends at a locked gate. There is a trail beside the creek for 1.0 mile to a hiking club cabin, and from that point the Porters Creek Trail follows the stream for 2.7 more miles. Small streams with fishable waters include: Boulevard Creek (1.5 miles), Cannon Creek (1.5), False Gap Creek (2.8), Long Branch (2.4), Kalanu Prong (1.5), Lowes Creek (1.5), and Shultz Prong (1.2) miles.

Many anglers seek streams off the beaten path. Here a pair of fishermen get set to walk to a high-elevation tributary of a major park stream.

10

Pigeon River Drainage

COSBY CREEK

Location: Northeast section

Fishable miles: 3.8

Quads: Hartford, Luftee Knob

Predominant species: Rainbow and brook trout

Quality of fishing: Fair

Comments: This is a small stream that gets a lot of pressure from local anglers, but there is some good brook trout fishing in the upper reaches.

Best flies: Small nymphs (Black Stone, Dark-Cream Caddis Pupa, and Pheasant Tail, sizes 14 to 20, and Blue-Winged Olive, March Brown, and Yellow Elk-Hair Caddis, sizes 14 to 20) are good during the spring. Best in summer and fall are a variety of attractor flies (Tennessee Wulff, Yellow and Green Humpy, and Orange Palmer, sizes 10 to 14), nymphs (Tellico, Hare's Ear, and Secret Weapon, sizes 10 to 14), and terrestrials (Chartreuse Inchworm, Deer-Hair Ant, and Bullet-Head Grasshoppers, sizes 10 to 16).

Access: Cosby Creek is accessible on the Cosby Campground Road that turns right from TN 32 east of Cosby adjacent to the park boundary. The road follows the Cosby Creek to the campground. A trail that begins at the campground travels along the stream for less than a mile. Small streams with fishable waters include: Crying Creek (3.1 miles), Fletcher Springs Branch (0.8), and Inadu Creek (1.3).

Closed: Toms Creek and Rock Creek are closed to fishing, as is Cosby Creek above where the Low Gap Trail crosses the stream. Refer to the *Restricted Waters* map at the back of the book and the master list in chapter 2.

BIG CREEK

Location: Northeast section

Fishable miles: 11.0 miles

Quads: Waterville, Cove Creek, Luftee Knob

Predominant species: Rainbow trout

Quality of fishing: Excellent

Comments: The entire creek offers exceptionally fine fishing, but it has a strong current and is difficult to wade. The most productive parts of the creek are the portion on the lower end near the ranger station, above and below Mouse Creek Falls and the "Blue Hole" (which can't be missed), and above the Walnut Bottoms campground. Note: This is an area often frequented by bears.

Best flies: In winter nymphs (Hare's Ear, Pheasant Tail, and Yellow Stonefly Creeper, sizes 14 to 20) are good. In spring and into summer dry flies (Thunderhead, Female Olive Caddis, and Adams, sizes 12 to 18) and nymphs (Peacock Wooly Worm, Prince, and Pheasant Tail, sizes 12 to 16) work well. Favorites in late summer and early fall are bushy attractor flies (Royal Wulff, Carolina Wulff, and Yellow Palmer, sizes 10 to 14) and terrestrials (Bullet-Head Grasshopper, Green or Yellow Inchworm, and

Jungle Cock Jassid, sizes 10 to 22). Winter fishing is restricted mostly to tiny dry flies (Blue-Winged Olive, Griffith's Gnat, and Black Midge, sizes 18 to 22) and nymphs (Black Stone, Pheasant Tail, and Grey Caddis Pupa, sizes 16 to 22).

Access: There are two ways to access Big Creek. One is TN 32, which follows the park boundary from Cosby to the Big Creek Ranger Station. (Once past the Tennessee-North Carolina line, this highway becomes Old NC 284). The other is from I-40: Exit at 451, which is the Waterville Road. Cross the Pigeon River, then turn left and proceed 2.5 miles to an intersection. Go straight ahead past the Big Creek Ranger Station to the end of the road to a gate where the Big Creek Trail begins and follows the stream for 5.9 miles to Walnut Bottoms. Turn right at the junction with Gunter Creek Trail and follow for 1.0 mile to where Camel Gap Trail turns to the right. From that point the Camel Gap Trail follows Big Creek for 3.1 miles before turning right and ascending the ridge to the Appalachian Trail. Small streams with fishable waters include: Baxter Creek (2.0 miles), Bettis Creek (1.3), Chestnut Branch (3.4), and Swallow Fork.

Closed: Gunter Creek can be fished for 1.9 miles until the first trail crossing, and is closed beyond. Big Creek and Yellow Creek are closed above their junction, and McGinty Creek is closed at its junction with Swallow Fork. Refer to the *Restricted Waters* map at the end of the book and the master list in chapter 2.

Signs like this along a trail indicate that a campsite lies ahead.

CATALOOCHEE CREEK

Location: Southeast section

Fishable miles: 12.0

Quads: Dellwood, Cove Creek, Bunches Bald, Luftee Knob

Predominant species: Rainbow, brown, and brook trout

Quality of fishing: Poor to excellent—this stream can humble an angler like no other in the park.

Comments: This is definitely the easiest stream in the park to wade, made so by the topography of the cove. Strangely, and unexplainably, it is also the most variable. You have either a really good day or a fishless one. Through the summer months the cove portion offers good dry fly fishing, and in the fall the upper parts of Palmer Creek and Rough Fork are excellent for spawning brown trout.

Best flies: Streamers (Muddler Minnow, Woolly Bugger, and Black Ghost, sizes 6 to 10), very small dry flies (Blue Dun Thorax, Blue-Winged Olive, and Parachute Adams, sizes 14 to 22), and nymphs (Hare's Ear, Dark-Green Caddis Pupa, and Yellow Stonefly Creeper, sizes 14 to 20) are good choices in winter and early spring. Dry flies (Light Cahill, Adams, and Royal Wulff, sizes 12 to 16) and nymphs (Sheep Fly, Prince, and Yellow Stone, sizes 10 to 16) are best in late spring and early summer. In late summer and fall large attractor flies (Orange Palmer, Carolina Wulff, and Yellow Hammer) and terrestrials (Chartreuse Inchworm, Fur Ant, and Joe's Hopper, sizes 10 to 18) will be the most likely to put fish in the creel.

Access: There are two ways to access Cataloochee Creek, the shortest of which is to exit I-40 at exit 20 to NC 276. Turn right and go west to Cove Creek Road, then turn left and drive north approximately 4.0 miles on a winding dirt road to where the 3.9-mile paved Cataloochee Road travels through the valley and comes to a dead end at the junction of Palmer Creek and Rough Fork Creek. The other access is to follow Old NC 284 past the Big Creek Campground Road across Mt. Sterling Gap and on to Cataloochee Creek. This is also a long and twisting dirt road and nearly three times the length of the other access just described. However, it crosses Little Cataloochee Creek near its confluence with Cataloochee, from which there is no maintained trail the rest of the distance downstream to the park boundary. The road also parallels an approximately 2.0-mile-long gorge that provides a rugged fishing experience. The major tributaries are Caldwell Fork, Palmer Creek, Little Cataloochee Creek, and Rough Creek. Small streams with fishable waters include: Mossy Branch (1.8 miles), Lower Double Branch (0.8), and Winding Stair Branch (0.7).

Caldwell Fork

Fishable miles: 7.2

Quads: Cove Creek, Bunches Bald

Predominant species: Rainbow and brown trout

Quality of fishing: Fair to good

Access: Caldwell Fork is accessible from the paved road where it enters Cataloochee Creek. The Caldwell Fork Trail follows the stream for nearly 5.0 miles. From that point upstream there is no maintained trail. Small streams with fishable water include: Den Branch (1.9 miles), Double Gap Branch (0.9), McKee Creek (1.4), Snake Branch (1.1), and Straight Creek (1.3).

Palmer Creek

Fishable miles: 4.5

Quads: Cove Creek, Luftee Knob

Predominant species: Rainbow trout, with brook trout at elevation

Quality of fishing: Excellent fall fishery

Access: Palmer Creek comes in from the right at the western end of Cataloochee Road. A trail begins here and follows the creek almost to its end. Little Cataloochee Trail goes to the right at 0.8 mile, and 0.5 mile ahead Pretty Hollow Creek comes in from the right. This is Palmer Creek's major tributary, with 2.8 miles of fishable water; a small feeder branch, Cook Creek, has 1.4 miles. Only one small stream on Palmer Creek, Beech Creek, has 2.7 miles of fishable water.

Closed: Lost Bottom Creek is closed to fishing from its confluence with Palmer Creek. Refer to the *Restricted Waters* map at the end of the book and the master list in chapter 2.

Little Cataloochee Creek

Fishable miles: 2.5

Quad: Cove Creek

Predominant species: Rainbow and brown trout

Quality of fishing: Good

Access: There is auto access from Old NC 284 to Little Cataloochee Creek only a short distance north of its confluence with Cataloochee Creek. A marked path that crosses Correll Creek leads 1.0 mile to Little Cataloochee Trail, which makes its only contact with Little Cataloochee Creek 0.2 mile south. There is no maintained trail along the creek. Small streams with fishable waters include: Andy Branch (1.4 miles), Coggins Creek (1.8), and Conrad Branch (0.7).

Deep Creek near Bryson City, North Carolina, is one of the most popular park streams, but the best fishing is in the waters that require a lengthy hike to reach.

Rough Fork

Fishable miles: 4.3

Quads: Dellwood, Bunches Bald

Predominant species: Rainbow trout

Quality of fishing: Good spring and fall fishery

Access: The Old Palmer Chapel Road turns left at the west end of Cataloochee Road and follows upstream for 1.0 mile. Rough Fork Trail begins at the end of the road and parallels the stream for an additional 3.0 miles. At this point the creek turns right and there is no maintained trail upstream. Small streams with fishable waters include: Messer Fork (1.3 miles), Shanty Branch (1.8), and Woody Creek (1.3).

Highway 441 parallels the Oconaluftee River on the North Carolina side of the park for almost all of its length.

11

Oconaluftee River System

OCONALUFTEE RIVER

Location: Central to Southeast section

Fishable miles: 12.8

Quads: Smokemont, Clingmans Dome

Predominant species: Rainbow and brown trout

Quality of fishing: Fair in early season; good to excellent in late season

Comments: Part of this river and some of its tributaries lie within the Cherokee Indian Reservation, which stocks the waters they control. As a result, some of the larger fish migrate up into the park, especially in the fall when the brown trout are on the move. Taking an occasional smallmouth in the river isn't unusual. Some favorite spots are in the vicinity of Kephart Prong and where Collins Creek and Bradley Fork enter.

Best flies: The streams of the Oconaluftee River System are where the Thunderhead and Yellow Hammer flies gained fame, so they are standards for both local and visiting anglers. Winter and early spring preferences are streamers (Black Ghost, Muddler Minnow, and Woolly Bugger, sizes 6 to 8), small nymphs (Black Stone, Pheasant Tail, and Quill Gordon), and tiny dry flies (Blue-Winged Olive, Blue Dun Thorax, and Parachute Adams, sizes 18 to 22). Dry flies (Thunderhead,

Yellow Hammer, and Carolina Wulff, sizes 14 to 16) and nymphs (Yellow Stone, Peacock Wooly Worm, and Sheep Fly, sizes 10 to 12) are good summer choices. Top late-summer and fall favorites are large attractor dry flies (Orange Palmer, Chartreuse or Yellow Elk-Hair Caddis, and Light Cahill, sizes 10 to 14) and terrestrials (Joe's Hopper, Yellow Inchworm, and Letort Cricket, sizes 12 to 14). Terrestrial patterns are particularly productive on the lower reaches where large, open fields border the river.

Access: The Oconaluftee River, like the Little Pigeon River on the opposite side of the park, is accessible by auto on US 441 for much of its length. There are many parking areas directly beside the river and numerous trails that lead to or follow alongside it. Even after the stream is no longer visible from the road, a walk of a few minutes duration along one of these paths will take the fisherman to streamside. The major tributaries are Raven Fork, Straight Fork, and Bradley Fork. Smaller streams with fishable water include: Aden Branch (1.4 miles), Becks Creek (2.0), Collins Creek (2.9), Couches Creek (1.3), Huskey Creek (1.1), Kephart Prong (2.2), and Tow String Branch (1.2). (Kephart Prong was once the site of a National Park Service fish hatchery, and Harry Middleton waxes eloquent on Collins Creek in his memorable book *On the Spine of Time* [Simon & Schuster, 1991].) The upper portion of the Oconaluftee is sometimes referred to as Beech Flats Prong, but it is simply an extension of the main river.

Raven Fork

Fishable miles: 10.0

Quads: Smokemont, Mt. Guyot, Luftee Knob

Predominant species: Brook and rainbow trout

Quality of fishing: Excellent

Comments: This stream is a favorite with veteran fly fishermen. It flows out of one of the park's best-preserved and most rugged wilderness areas, and its swift, challenging waters deter less hardy anglers. Also, it offers the best brook trout fishing in the entire park, and this species vastly outnumbers rainbows. Favorite stretches are the first 1.0 mile upstream from the park boundary near the end of the Big Cove Road loop and the upper waters above and below where Enloe Creek (which is closed) enters the stream.

Best flies: Brookies actively swat tiny dry flies (Dark Caddis, Blue Dun Thorax, and Blue-Winged Olive, sizes 18 to 22) in winter and early spring months, and small nymphs (Black Stone, Pheasant Tail, and Grey Caddis Pupa, sizes 18 to 22) in spring and summer. Dry flies (Black and Chartreuse Elk-Hair Caddis, and Thunderhead, sizes 12 to 16) are ideal for the turbulent water in this stream. Large nymphs (Golden Stone, Black Stone, and Hare's Ear, sizes 10 to 14) are also good. In late summer and early fall attractor dry flies (Royal Wulff, Yellow Hammer, and Orange Palmer, sizes 10 to 14) produce well, as do terrestrials (Bullet-Head Grasshopper, Chartreuse Inchworm, and Fur Ant, sizes 12 to 14).

Access: Raven Fork is a paradox in that one portion of it offers auto access and another part only foot access. The latter is in wilderness country with only a rudimentary trail system. The road access is Big Cove Road, which begins close to the park boundary. Approximately 1.1 miles of the stream are with-

An angler prepares to release a rainbow trout, a species that was introduced into the Smokies when brook trout habitat was destroyed.

in easy reach until the road enters the Cherokee Indian Reservation. Continue for approximately 9.0 miles on Big Cove Road past Straight Fork Road. At the northern end of the Big Cove Road the park boundary is only a few hundred yards upstream on Raven Fork. There is no maintained trail anywhere along the stream. An alternate plan is to drive up Straight Fork Road to the Hyatt Ridge Trail. Follow it for 1.9 miles to the junction with Enloe Creek Trail. Turn left and the trail crosses Raven Fork 1.0 farther just above where Enloe Creek enters Raven Fork. The trail then parallels Enloe Creek for another 1.3 miles. This plan allows the best access to the upper waters of the stream. Smaller streams with fishable water include: Redman Creek (3.3 miles) and Heintooga Creek (1.0).

Closed: Stillwell Creek and Bunches Creek are closed at the park boundary, Enloe Creek is closed at the junction with Raven Fork, and Raven Fork is closed at Big Pool, which is the confluence of Left Fork, Middle Fork, and Right Fork. Refer to the *Restricted Waters* map at the back of the book and the master list in chapter 2.

Straight Fork

Fishable miles: 6.5

Quads: Bunches Bald, Luftee Knob

Predominant species: Rainbow and brook trout

Quality of fishing: Fair to good

Comments: This stream does not get a lot of pressure from visiting anglers, and it can be a sleeper that is worth investigating. There is road access to the Round Bottom Picnic Area and beyond, but by hiking upstream from this spot there is plenty of water to explore.

Best flies: Small dry fly patterns (Blue-Winged Olive, Quill

Gordon, and March Brown, sizes 18 to 22) do well, as well as tiny nymphs (Griffith's Gnat, Blue Dun Thorax, and Light Hendrickson, sizes 16 to 20). For summer fishing dry flies (Adams, Green and Yellow Humpies, and Cream Elk Caddis, sizes 12 to 16) and nymphs (Yellow Caddis Pupa, Green Stone, and Sheep Fly, sizes 10 to 16) pay off. Good choices for summer and fall are large attractor dry flies (Carolina Wulff, Orange Palmer, and Yellow Hammer, sizes 10 to 14), and terrestrials (Bullet-Head Grasshopper, Green Inchworm, and Deer-Hair Ant, sizes 10 to 18).

Access: The Round Bottom Road, which turns right off the Big Cove Road in the Cherokee Reservation, follows Straight Fork for 3.8 miles from the park boundary to the Round Bottom Picnic Ground, and there is easy auto access the entire distance. From the picnic ground there is no maintained trail the rest of the way up the stream. Small streams with fishable water include: Ledge Creek (1.6 miles) and Round Bottom Creek (0.8).

Closed: Straight Fork and Balsam Creek are closed at their common junction. Refer to the *Restricted Waters* map at the back of the book and the master list in chapter 2.

Bradley Fork

Fishable miles: 8.5

Quad: Smokemont, Mt. Guyot

Predominant species: Rainbow, brown, and brook trout

Quality of fishing: Excellent fall fishery

Comments: Bradley Fork is well known to fly fishermen who frequent park waters due to the good population of large browns and rainbows. It is a favorite among local fishermen, and easy access to the lower reaches of the stream from the

Smokemont Campground creates a lot of competition, particularly in the summer. However, those willing to do a little walking can escape the crowds and enjoy the excellent waters that lie upstream, particularly above where Chasteen Creek enters the stream. In fact, Chasteen Creek, while tiny and requiring the right equipment for close-quarters fishing, is worth fishing up through the horse camp.

Best flies: This stream has a healthy aquatic insect population. In winter and early spring very small dry flies (Dark Caddis, Black or Grey Midge, and Blue-Winged Olive, sizes 18 to 22) and nymphs (Black Stone, Herl Gordon, and Grey Caddis Pupa, sizes 18 to 22) get results. Late spring and summer offer some of the most impressive hatches of large mayflies seen anywhere in the park. Green Drakes in sizes 10 to 12 are readily accepted. Other dry flies (Adams, Thunderhead, and Light Cahill, sizes 10 to 14) are also popular, along with nymphs (Golden Stone, Woolly Bugger, and My Pet, sizes 10 to 14). Big dry flies (Royal Wulff, Yellow Hammer, and Orange Palmer, sizes 10 to 14) work well in late summer and fall months, and various terrestrials (Dave's Hopper, Chartreuse Inchworm, and Jungle Cock Jassid, sizes 18 to 22) can bring good rewards.

Access: A short portion of Bradley Fork is accessible by auto along the Smokemont Campground Road off US 441 approximately 4.0 miles north of the park boundary. The Bradley Fork Trail begins at the north end of the campground and follows the stream for 4.1 miles to a turn-around in the trail. At this point the Bradley Fork Trail ends and Dry Sluice Gap Trail and Cabin Flats Trail begin. Bradley Fork swings to the right and flows beside Cabin Flats Trail 1.1 miles to a campground. An unmaintained trail follows Bradley Fork for the

128   remaining 1.1 miles of open water. Smaller streams with fishable waters include: Chasteen Creek (3.5 miles), Tennessee Branch (2.0), and Louis Camp Prong (1.1).

Closed: Taywa Creek is closed at its junction with Bradley Fork, and Chasam Prong and Gulf Prong are closed at their common junction with Bradley Fork. Refer to the *Restricted Waters* map at the back of the book and the master list in chapter 2.

12

Little Tennessee River Drainage

DEEP CREEK

Location: South-Central section

Fishable miles: 13.0

Quads: Bryson City and Clingmans Dome

Predominant species: Rainbow and brown trout, with brook trout at higher elevations

Quality of fishing: Good to excellent

Comments: This is one of the few streams in the park where a grand slam of rainbow, browns, and brooks can be scored. It is popular and well known to both locals and visiting anglers, but the amount of water the main stream and the tributaries provide makes it possible to find plenty of privacy. All of the best water lies above Indian Creek Falls (at least in the summer months when tourists can rent innertubes and float the creek from this point down, creating an intolerable situation for fly fishermen). Favorite spots are those at least 1.0 mile above Indian Creek Falls and the very upper reaches of the stream.

Best flies: In early season small- to medium-size dry flies (March Brown, Adams, and Dark Caddis, sizes 12 to 18) are good, and nymphs (Black Stone, Pheasant Tail, and Hare's Ear, sizes 12 to 18) are dependable. In summer large dry flies (Elk-Hair Caddis, Royal Wulff, and Thunderhead, sizes 10 to 14) and big nymphs (Golden Stone, Prince and My Pet, sizes 8-14) yield good results. These same flies are suitable into the fall, along with terrestrials (Chartreuse Inchworm, Joe's Hopper, and Fur Ant, sizes 12 to 8). Some big browns move into the lower reaches of Deep Creek in the late fall and winter and can be taken on streamers (Grey Ghost, Woolly Bugger, and Muddler Minnow and various egg patterns).

Access: Take the Deep Creek Campground Road from Bryson City to the campground, from which there is auto access to a gate 0.5 mile above the campground. At this point the Deep Creek Trail begins and basically follows the stream and its right fork for approximately 10.0 miles to the junction with Fork Ridge Trail. Beyond this point, the Deep Creek Trail remains parallel to the creek, although elevated high above it and not always providing easy access. No maintained trail follows the creek above the Deep Creek-Fork Ridge trail junction. Also, there is access to the upper end of the creek from a trailhead near Newfound Gap that drops from high elevation to the Poke Patch campsite. The hike back out is very difficult and should be attempted only by anglers in good physical shape. Deep Creek's main tributaries are Indian Creek, Pole Road Creek, Rocky Fork, Left Fork, and Beetree Creek. Smaller streams with fishable water include: Bridge Creek (1.4 miles), Cherry Creek (1.3), Hammer Branch (0.9), and Nettle Creek (1.8).

Closed: Sahlee Creek is closed to fishing at its confluence with Deep Creek. Refer to the *Restricted Waters* map at the back of the book and the master list in chapter 2.

Indian Creek

Fishable miles: 6.3

Quads: Bryson City, Clingmans Dome

Predominant species: Rainbow trout

Quality of fishing: Fair

Access: The Indian Branch Trail turns right off the Deep Creek Trail less than 1.0 mile past the locked gate. The trail follows the creek for 4.0 miles, and at approximately 3.0 miles the Deeplow Trail turns right and follows George's Branch for 1.0 mile. There is no maintained trail beyond this point.

Pole Road Creek

Fishable miles: 1.3

Quad: Clingmans Dome

Predominant species: Rainbow trout

Quality of fishing: Fair

Access: Pole Road Creek enters Deep Creek from the left 6.8 miles from the beginning of Deep Creek Trail. Pole Road Trail follows the creek for almost its entire length.

Rocky Fork

Fishable miles: 3.2

Quad: Clingmans Dome

Predominant species: Brook trout

Quality of fishing: Excellent

Access: Rocky Fork enters Deep Creek from the left 10.3 miles upstream from where the Deep Creek Trail terminates above Deep Creek Campground. The trailhead begins on the Newfound Gap Road 1.7 miles south of Newfound Gap, and from that end the hike down to Rocky Fork is less than 4.0 miles. There is no maintained trail along the creek.

This 1,200-foot tunnel marks the end of a highway that was intended to border the south side of the park. It was halted for environmental reasons.

Left Fork

Fishable miles: 6.2

Quad: Clingmans Dome

Predominant species: Rainbow trout

Quality of fishing: Very good

Access: Left Fork enters Deep Creek on the left 0.5 mile past Pole Road Creek Trail. There is no maintained trail along the creek. This stream is particularly prone to sudden floods due to cloudbursts. Small streams with fishable water include: Bear Pen Branch (1.5 miles) and Keg Drive Branch (1.5).

Beetree Creek

Fishable miles: 2.0

Quad: Clingmans Dome

Predominant species: Brook trout

Access: Beetree Creek enters Deep Creek from the right 9.7 miles from the beginning of Deep Creek Trail. There is no maintained trail along the stream.

NOLAND CREEK

Location: South-Central section

Fishable miles: 10.5

Quads: Noland Creek, Bryson City, Clingmans Dome

Predominate species: Rainbow and brown trout

Quality of fishing: Good to excellent

Comments: Noland Creek is a relatively small stream that offers fine fly fishing opportunity. It runs down through a narrow and heavily forested area that isn't heavily frequented by anglers, and hikes of a mile or more upstream can be very rewarding in terms of finding privacy and isolation. There are also brook trout at the higher elevations. Favorite spots are just as described: upstream and the farther the better.

Best flies: Small dark dry flies (Blue Dun Thorax, Blue-Winged Olive, and Quill Gordon, sizes 18 to 22) are good in winter and early spring, along with nymphs (Black Stone, Hare's Ear, and Pheasant Tail, sizes 16 to 20). In summer larger dry flies (Light Cahill, Thunderhead, and Adams, sizes 10 to 14) and nymphs (Golden Stone, My Pet, and Prince, sizes 10 to 14) are preferred. Large attractor flies (Carolina Wulff, Orange Palmer, and Yellow Hammer, sizes 10 to 14) and terrestrials (Bullet-Head Grasshopper, Deer Hair, and Yellow Inchworm, sizes 10 to 14) are good fall picks.

Access: Noland Creek passes under the Lakeview Drive (also known as "The Road to Nowhere") 7.0 miles from Bryson City. The Noland Creek Trail, which begins south of the bridge over the stream on Lakeview Drive, follows the creek from Fontana Lake for 10.0 miles to the Noland Divide Trail. Noland Creek's main tributaries are Laurel Creek, Bearpen Branch, and Mill Creek. Small streams with fishable water include: Indian Creek (0.9 mile) and Springhouse Branch (0.6).

Closed: Noland Creek and Salola Branch are closed upstream from their confluence. Refer to the *Restricted Waters* map at the back of the book and the master list in chapter 2.

Laurel Creek

Fishable miles: 1.5

Quad: Noland Creek

Predominant species: Rainbow trout

Quality of fishing: Good

Access: Laurel Creek enters Noland Creek from the left just south of the bridge on Lakeview Drive. There is no maintained trail along the stream.

Mill Creek

Fishable miles: 1.6

Quads: Noland Creek, Clingmans Dome

Predominant species: Rainbow trout

Quality of fishing: Good

Access: Mill Creek flows into Noland Creek from the left 4.2 miles from the trailhead at the junction of Noland Creek Trail and Springhouse Branch Trail. The Springhouse Branch Trail follows the stream for approximately 0.5 mile.

FORNEY CREEK

Location: South-Central section

Fishable miles: 9.0

Quads: Noland Creek, Silers Bald

Predominant species: Rainbow and brown trout

Quality of fishing: Fair to good

Comments: Forney Creek offers a haven for those who find some of its sister streams too crowded, and in places it can be a productive and pleasant stream to fish. However, the stream bed is narrow, and the spring floods of 1993 made portions of

Big waters that are swift and deep are where a wading staff can make the difference in staying dry and getting wet.

the creek all but impassable due to fallen trees and debris. Also, it has a swift current and extremely slick rocks.

Best flies: Basically the same as those recommended for Noland Creek since they are in close proximity. Brown trout also invade this creek in the fall and winter months, so it is a good choice for anglers who like to fish streamers and egg patterns in the off season.

Access: The easiest access to Forney Creek is by boat from Wilderness Marina on Fontana Lake. The Forney Creek Trail begins just above where the creek flows into the lake and follows the stream for 8.1 miles. It can also be reached from the Lakeshore Trail that begins at the end of Lakeview Road. The distance to the creek is 3.3 miles. At 2.2 miles the Whiteoak Branch Trail branches off to the right and joins the Forney Creek Trail 2.0 miles farther upstream. The main tributaries are Bear Creek, Bee Gum Branch, Jonas Creek, Slab Camp Creek, and White Mans Glory Creek. Small streams with fishable water include: Advalorem Branch (0.8 mile), Board Camp Creek (1.2), Choke Berry Branch (1.0), Little Jonas Creek (1.4), Scarlet Ridge Creek (1.8), Steeltrap Branch (1.6), and Woody Creek (1.0).

Closed: Huggins Creek is closed at the cascades. Refer to the *Restricted Waters* map at the end of the book and the master list in chapter 2.

Bear Creek

Fishable miles: 2.9

Quad: Noland Creek

Predominant species: Rainbow trout

Quality of fishing: Fair to good

Access: Bear Creek enters Forney Creek 1.0 mile upstream from Fontana Lake at the junction of Bear Creek Trail and

Forney Creek Trail. The Bear Creek Trail follows the stream for 2.8 miles, then bears right. There is no maintained trail further up the creek.

Bee Gum Branch

Fishable miles: 1.6

Quad: Noland Creek

Predominant species: Rainbow trout

Quality of fishing: Fair

Access: Bear Creek enters Forney Creek from the right 2.0 miles upstream from the Bear Creek Trail, and the Springhouse Branch Trail follows it intermittently for most of its fishable length.

Jonas Creek

Fishable miles: 3.2

Quad: Silers Bald

Predominant species: Rainbow trout

Quality of fishing: Fair

Access: The confluence of Jonas Creek with Forney Creek is 4.2 miles up Forney Creek Trail. The Jonas Creek Trail begins at this point and follows Jonas Creek for 1.2 miles to where Little Jonas Creek enters from the left. The trail then runs parallel to Little Jonas Creek for 0.5 mile. There is no maintained trail above where Jonas Creek Trail departs the main stream.

Slab Camp Creek

Fishable miles: 2.1

Quad: Noland Creek

Predominant species: Rainbow and brook trout

Quality of fishing: Fair to good

Access: Slab Camp Creek flows into Forney Creek from the left 0.5 mile beyond Bee Gum Creek on the Forney Creek Trail. There is no maintained trail along the stream.

White Mans Glory Creek

Fishable miles: 2.3

Quad: Noland Creek

Predominant species: Rainbow trout

Quality of fishing: Fair to good

Access: White Mans Glory Creek comes into Forney Creek from the left 0.4 mile beyond Slab Camp Creek on the Forney Creek Trail. There is no maintained trail along the stream.

CHAMBERS CREEK

Location: South-Central section

Fishable miles: 4.5

Quad: Noland Creek

Predominant species: Rainbow trout

Quality of fishing: Fair to poor

Comments: There is very little fishing water in Chambers Creek, and except for those who place privacy over the prospects of enjoying some action on the water, there are far better choices elsewhere.

Access: A boat ride up Fontana Lake from Fontana Village Marina (828-498-2211, extension 277), either of the two U.S. Forest Service campgrounds, or one of the several docks closer to the headwaters provides the easiest access to Chambers Creek, which can also be reached on the Lakeshore Trail between Forney Creek and Hazel Creek. There is an unmaintained trail up the creek that leads to where the West and North Fork join, and streamside anglers' paths run for a short distance beside both of these small streams.

HAZEL CREEK

Location: Southwest section

Fishable miles: 11.0

Quads: Tuskeegee, Thunderhead, Silers Bald

Predominant species: Rainbow and brown trout, with brook trout at the higher elevations

Quality of fishing: Very good

Comments: Hazel Creek is probably the most famous stream in the park, and even though accessible only by boat or on foot, it nevertheless gets an enormous amount of attention from visiting anglers. The creek deserves the accolades it has been given, because it is a beautiful and productive stream in an historic setting. Favorite spots are the lower reaches that are commonly bypassed by fishermen and the portion in and beyond Bone Valley. There are numerous productive tributaries.

Best flies: Because big browns enter the lower reaches of the stream in the winter, streamers (Mickey Finn, Grey Ghost, and Muddler Minnow, sizes 8 to 12) are very effective. Late winter and early spring have hatches of very small dry flies (Black Midge, Blue-Winged Olive, and Parachute Adams, sizes 16 to 22), and trout are feeding on nymphs (Black Stone, Grey Caddis Pupa, and Pheasant Tail, sizes 16 to 22). There are good fly hatches in summer (Thunderhead, Black Elk-Hair Caddis, and Adams, sizes 12 to 16), and good nymph activity (Golden Stone, Sheep Fly, and

Cream Caddis Pupa, sizes 14 to 16). Late-summer and fall anglers favor attractor flies (Royal Wulff, Orange Palmer, and Yellow Hammer, sizes 10 to 14) and terrestrials (Dave's Hopper, Deer Hair Ant, and Chartreuse Inchworm, sizes 10 to 14).

Access: The boat shuttle across Fontana Lake from Fontana Village Marina is the only access to the mouth except the Lakeshore Trail between Chambers Creek and Eagle Creek. The Lakeshore Trail follows the creek upstream for 4.7 miles to Sugar Fork, where it turns left. At this point the Hazel Creek Trail begins and follows the stream to the end of the fishable water. The main tributaries are Bone Valley Creek, Sugar Fork, and Proctor Creek. Small streams with fishable miles include: Cold Springs Branch (1.9 miles), Little Huggins Branch (0.6), Elbow Branch (0.6), and Hawk Ridge Branch.

Closed: Walkers Creek is closed to fishing at the falls, Defeat Creek at the junction with Bone Valley Creek, and Hazel Creek at the cascades. Refer to the *Restricted Waters* map at the end of the book and the master list in chapter 2.

Bone Valley Creek

Fishable miles: 4.7

Quads: Tuskeegee, Thunderhead

Predominant species: Rainbow and brook trout

Quality of fishing: Excellent

Access: The Bone Valley Trail turns left off Hazel Creek Trail 5.4 miles from Fontana Lake and follows the stream for 1.8 miles to a dead end. There is an unmaintained trail beyond this point that provides upstream access to some small streams with fishable water that include: Wooly Ridge Creek (1.2 miles), Desolation Creek (1.6), Calhoun Branch (0.7), and Nunda Branch (1.5).

All springs and streams in the park are considered to be polluted, and drinking from them is not advised. Small water purification units that filter *Giardia* make the water safe.

Sugar Fork

Fishable miles: 1.8

Quads: Tuskeegee, Thunderhead

Predominant species: Rainbow trout

Quality of fishing: Fair to good

Access: The Lakeshore Trail follows Sugar Fork almost to its end. At 0.5 mile up the trail Haw Gap Branch enters Sugar Fork, and an unmaintained trail follows this tributary for much of the stream's length of fishable water.

Proctor Creek

Fishable miles: 3.1

Quad: Silers Bald

Predominant species: Rainbow and brook trout

Quality of fishing: Excellent

Access: Proctor Creek joins Hazel Creek from the left roughly 10 miles from Fontana Lake. There is an unmaintained trail that follows the creek upstream from this confluence.

EAGLE CREEK

Location: Southwest section

Fishable miles: 7.1

Predominant species: Rainbow trout

Quality of fishing: Excellent

Comments: Eagle Creek lies in close proximity to Hazel Creek, but it has escaped the large influx of anglers and offers a very fine experience for the angler. The stream is of medium size, but in progressing up it one encounters deep, emerald-colored pools and long runs that can't be passed without making a few casts, regardless of your ultimate destination. The upper waters provide the most action, but the lower reaches hold trout of bragging size that require some expertise to entice into striking. Favorite spots are from where Ekaneetlee Creek enters.

Best flies: Winter or early spring activity is minimal, with occasional hatches of tiny flies (Blue-Winged Olives, Blue Dun Thorax, and Black Midge, sizes 18 to 22). Small nymphs (Black Stone, Grey Caddis Pupa, and Pheasant Tail, sizes 18 to 22) will get results during feeding periods. Favored in summer are dry flies (Black Elk-Hair Caddis, Adams, and Thunderhead, sizes 12 to 16) and nymphs (Brown Stone, Cream Caddis Pupa, and Sheep Fly, sizes 12 to 16). In late summer and fall attractor flies (Royal Wulff, Yellow Hammer, and Orange Palmer, size 10 to 14), have strong appeal, and terrestrials (Bullet-Head Grasshopper, Fur Ant, and Jungle Cock Jassids, sizes 10 to 22) share the spotlight.

Quads: Fontana Dam, Cades Cove, Thunderhead Mountain

Access: The two routes to Eagle Creek are either to hike in from Fontana Dam on the Lakeshore Trail for 6.2 miles or to travel by boat from Fontana Village Marina. The Lakeshore Trail follows beside the stream for 0.8 mile to where the Eagle Creek Trail begins and follows the creek to its uppermost waters. The main tributaries are Lost Cove Creek (which actually flows into Fontana Lake when at full pool), Pinnacle Creek, Ekaneetlee Creek, and Tub Mill Creek. Small streams with fishable miles include: Camp Ten Branch (0.8 mile) and Paw Paw Creek (1.6).

Closed: Gunna Creek is closed to fishing at trail crossing at 3,080-foot elevation. Refer to the *Restricted Waters* map at the end of the book and the master list in chapter 2.

Lost Cove Creek

Fishable miles: 2.4

Quad: Fontana Dam

Predominant species: Rainbow trout

Quality of fishing: Fair to good

Access: Lost Cove Creek enters the creek—or lake, depending on lake level—from the left, and the Lost Cove Trail begins there and follows the stream for its fishable length.

Pinnacle Creek

Fishable miles: 5.0

Quads: Fontana Dam, Thunderhead Mountain

Predominant species: Rainbow trout

Quality of fishing: Fair

Access: Pinnacle Creek joins Eagle Creek at the junction of the Lakeshore and Eagle Creek Trails. The Lakeshore Trail travels beside or near Pinnacle Creek for nearly 3.0 miles. From that point there is no maintained trail beside the stream.

Ekaneetlee Creek

Fishable miles: 5.0

Quads: Fontana Dam, Cades Cove, Tuskeegee

Predominant species: Rainbow trout

Quality of fishing: Good to excellent

Access: Ekaneetlee Creek enters Eagle Creek 0.8 mile from the Eagle Creek trailhead. There is an unmaintained trail that follows the stream for most of its length.

Tub Mill Creek

Fishable miles: 2.1

Quad: Cades Cove

Predominant species: Rainbow trout

Quality of fishing: Fair

Access: Tub Mill and Gunna Creek join 4.5 miles from the Eagle Creek trailhead. There is no maintained trail up Tub Mill Creek.

TWENTYMILE CREEK

Location: Southwest section

Fishable miles: 5.0

Quads: Tapoco, Fontana Dam

Predominant species: Rainbow and brown trout

Quality of fishing: Good spring and fall fishery

Comments: In the fall and spring low elevations of this creek hold large numbers of browns and rainbows migrating up from Cheoah Lake. This is an attractive stream, but most of the fish are small. Waters at the higher elevations are the most productive.

Best flies: Using Eagle Creek as an example will adequately define what to expect on this stream.

Access: There is auto access to the parking lot at the Twentymile Ranger Station just off NC 28 between Deals Gap and Fontana Village. At the locked gate a trail begins that forks 0.5 mile upstream, the left fork becoming the Wolf Ridge Trail and the right Twentymile Trail, which follows the creek for 3.0 miles to a junction with Long Hungry Ridge Trail. At this point the Twentymile Trail ends and the creek is paralleled for

another 1.1 miles by the Long Hungry Ridge Trail. The main
tributaries are Moore Springs Branch and Greer Creek. Small
streams with fishable miles include Proctor Cove Branch (0.5
mile) and Rye Patch Branch (0.5).

Moore Springs Branch

Fishable miles: 3.0

Quads: Fontana Dam, Cades Cove, Tapoco

Predominant species: Rainbow trout

Quality of fishing: Fair

Access: Moore Springs Branch enters Twentymile Creek
from the left 0.5 mile beyond the trailhead at the ranger station.
The Wolf Ridge Trail follows Moore Springs Branch for 1.0 mile
to the junction with the Twenty Mile Loop Trail. From that point
there is no maintained trail along the stream. A tributary, Dalton
Branch, has 1.8 miles of fishable water .

Greer Creek

Fishable water: 1.1

Quads: Fontana Dam, Cades Cove

Predominant species: Rainbow trout

Quality of fishing: Fair

Access: Greer Creek joins Twentymile Creek 3.0 miles from
the trailhead. There is no maintained trail along the stream
from this point.

Many of the trails paralleling streams are old railroad beds built by lumber companies before the park was established.

ABRAMS CREEK
(BELOW THE FALLS)

Location: Western section

Fishable miles: 14.0

Quads: Calderwood, Blockhouse, Kinzel Springs

Predominant species: Rainbow and brown trout, with small-mouths and redeyes at lower elevations

Quality of fishing: Good to excellent in spring and fall

Comments: This portion of Abrams Creek is subject to high water temperatures and low dissolved oxygen during the summer months, which makes for tough fishing. However, this is somewhat compensated for by the good spring runs of rainbow trout, as well as fall runs of brown trout out of Chilhowee Lake that produce some trophy fish. Favorite spots are the Little Bottoms upstream from the Abrams Creek Campground and the waters above this point that offer a series of excellent pools and riffles.

Best flies: The best winter and early spring action comes with streamers (Muddler Minnow, Woolly Bugger, and Grey Ghost, sizes 6 to 10) in the lower reaches where the big browns are concentrated. In the spring there are good hatches and dry flies (Black and Yellow Elk-Hair Caddis, Thunderhead, and Adams, sizes 12 to 16, and Green Drakes, sizes 8 to 10) are very effective. Nymphs (Golden Stone, Hare's Ear, and Pheasant Tail, sizes 12 to 16) are also eagerly accepted. As stated, the summer fishing is slow, but in the fall, big dry flies (Tennessee Wulff, Yellow Hammer, and Light Cahill, sizes 10 to 14) get lots of attention. Terrestrials (Yellow Inchworms, Joe's Hopper, and Deer-Hair Ant, sizes 10 to 14) are also good choices.

Access: The part of Abrams Creek from the Abrams Creek Campground to where it enters Chilhowee Lake is accessible only by following an unmaintained trail between the two locations. There is auto access by following the Happy Valley Road off US 129 to the Abrams Creek Campground. From the campground the Cooper Road Trail parallels Kingfisher Creek for 1.4 miles to the junction with Little Bottoms Trail, which turns right and in 2.3 miles reaches the junction where Abrams Creek Trail and Hannah Mountain Trail meet. Stay left on Abrams Creek Trail, which continues 4.2 miles to the falls (although not always in close proximity to the creek). The falls can also be reached from the Abrams Falls Trail that begins in Cades Cove between sign posts #10 and #11 on the Cades Cove Loop Road. The main tributaries on the lower section are Panther Creek and Rabbit Creek. Small streams with fishable water include: Andy McCully Branch (1.1 miles), Hannah Creek (1.4), Pardon Branch (1.1), Shoofly Branch (1.1), and Kingfisher Branch (1.5).

Panther Creek

Fishable miles: 9.6

Quad: Calderwood

Predominant species: Rainbow trout

Quality of fishing: Good to excellent

Access: Panther Creek enters the Abrams Creek embayment of Chilhowee from the right, and a hiking trail follows the stream for approximately 4.1 miles. From that point there is no further trail access to the stream until the one-way Parsons Branch Road crosses it 4.1 miles from where the road begins in Cades Cove. Small streams with fishable water include: Bear Den Branch (2.2 miles), Rollins Hollow (1.0), and Slaty Branch (0.9).

Rabbit Creek

Fishable miles: 7.7

Quad: Calderwood

Predominant species: Rainbow trout

Quality of fishing: Good early-season fishery

Access: Rabbit Creek enters Abrams Creek from the right at the point where Little Bottoms Trail, Hannah Mountain Trail, and Abrams Creek Trail meet, which is 3.7 miles from the Abrams Creek Campground. Another route is Rabbit Creek Jeep Road Trail, which turns left off the Abrams Falls Trailhead in Cades Cove just past the parking area and reaches Rabbit Creek at 2.5 miles beyond, approximately 0.5 mile upstream from its confluence with Abrams Creek. The Rabbit Creek Jeep Road Trail extends all the way to the Abrams Creek Campground near the park boundary. The upper portion of Rabbit Creek can be accessed on the Parson Branch Road 3.8 miles from its junction off the Cades Cove Loop Road. Small streams with fishable water include: Bell Cove Branch (1.6 miles) and Peckerwood Branch (1.4).

Q 41

HORACE KEPHART

— • • • —

Author of "Our Southern Highlanders" (1913) and other works, naturalist, librarian. Grave ³⁄10 mi. S. W. Mt. Kephart, 30 mi. N., is named for him.

Horace Kephart was one of the original supporters of the park movement. This marker is located in Bryson City, North Carolina, where he lived at the time of his death.

13

Cades Cove

ABRAMS CREEK
(ABOVE THE FALLS)

Location: Western section

Fishable miles: 8.9

Quads: Calderwood, Cades Cove, Kinzel Springs

Predominant species: Rainbow and brown trout

Quality of fishing: Good to excellent

Comments: As with the part of Abrams Creek below the falls, this is primarily a spring and fall fishery due to high temperatures generated in the open lands of Cades Cove that cause trout to become sluggish during the summer months. The difference is that it doesn't have the bonus of lake-run rainbows and browns. Favorite spots are the area between the falls and the cove, the best part of which is the horseshoe bend off the main trail and which requires a full day to fish. This waterway should not be traveled alone. The rocks in Abrams Creek are among the most slippery in the park, making the danger of an injury greater than at most other places.

Best flies: Streamers (Woolly Bugger, Muddler Minnow, and Black Ghost, sizes 6 to 10) work well in winter and early spring. Hatches also produce some action with dry flies (Black or Grey Midge, Blue-Winged Olive, and March Brown, sizes 14 to 22) effective, as well as nymphs (Grey Caddis Pupa, Black Stone, and Pheasant Tail, sizes 14 to 22). The cove has large pasture areas, and when fall action picks up terrestrials (Bullet-Head Grasshopper, Jungle Cock Jassid, and Yellow Inchworms, sizes 10 to 22) are exceptionally good. Also, large dry flies (Royal Wulff, Adams, and Thunderhead, sizes 10 to 14) produce well.

Access: There is access to Abrams Creek and several of its tributaries in Cades Cove by entering on the Laurel Creek Road that turns to the right off TN 73 at the Townsend Y just inside the park boundary. This becomes the Cades Cove Loop Road that circles the valley, and Abrams Creek (which is also called Anthony Creek in Cades Cove) flows through the area encompassed by the loop road. Two gravel roads that dissect the loop, Hyatt Lane and Sparks Lane, cross the creek, and there is easy access by foot for the entire length of the cove. The Abrams Creek Trail, which begins at the end of a dirt road that turns right off the loop road between sign posts #10 and #11, travels downstream to the falls for most of the 4.2 mile distance. The major exception is the wide excursion of the creek around a ridge that is known as "The Horseshoe." The main tributaries are Mill Creek and Forge Creek, which join just before emptying into Abrams Creek near where Abrams Falls Trail begins. Small streams with fishable water include: Arbutus Branch (2.2 miles), Rowans Creek (2.4), Stony Creek (1.5), Tater Branch (2.5), and Feezel Branch (2.2).

Mill Creek

Fishable miles: 4.0

Quad: Cades Cove

Predominant species: Rainbow trout

Quality of fishing: Good early-season fishery

Access: Mill Creek enters Abrams Creek from the right inside the cove and can be accessed by auto at the Abrams Falls parking area, the Becky Cable Historic House, and on Forge Creek Road. An unmaintained trail follows Mill Creek for 1.0 mile from the place where Forge Creek Road crosses it the second time. Its only feeder stream with fishable water is Wildcat Branch (0.9 mile).

Forge Creek

Fishable miles: 5.0

Quad: Cades Cove

Predominant species: Rainbow trout

Quality of fishing: Fair

Access: Forge Creek is accessible by auto for 2.0 miles on the Forge Creek Road, which turns right off the loop road just past the Cable Mill. At the place where the road leaves the creek, the Gregory Bald Trail follows the stream for another 1.9 miles before turning right and ascending the mountain. Beyond this point there is an unmaintained trail alongside the stream. Small streams with fishable water include Licking Branch (1.0 mile) and Ekaneetlee Branch (1.1).

Anglers prepare a streamside lunch of fresh rainbow trout near one of the old logging railroad bridges.

14

Other Smokies Streams

THERE ARE A FEW SMOKIES STREAMS NOT ASSOCIATED with major drainages or systems that offer good fishing opportunities and are worth including here.

TABCAT CREEK

Location: Western section

Fishable miles: 3.2

Quad: Calderwood

Predominant species: Rainbow trout

Quality of fishing: Fair

Access: Tabcat Creek flows into Calderwood Lake 2.5 miles south of the Abrams Creek embayment on US 129. An unmaintained trail follows the creek for more than 2.0 miles. Small streams with fishable waters include: Bunker Hill Creek (0.6 mile) and Maynard Creek (2.1).

HESSE CREEK

Location: Northwest section

Fishable miles: 5.5

Quads: Kinzel Springs

Predominant species: Rainbow trout

Quality of fishing: Good

Access: Hesse Creek is accessible by auto on the Miller Cove Road that turns right off US 321 between the Foothills Parkway and Kinzel Springs. The paved road ends after approximately 3.5 miles, and a gravel road turns right. A little over 0.5 mile farther a road turns to the left and follows Hesse Creek for a short distance until the road ends. From that point an unmaintained trail leads upstream to the park boundary and along the creek for most of its length. Other access is offered by the Cane Creek Trail and the Beard Cane Trail, both of which branch off the Cooper Road Trail that begins at the Abrams Creek Campground. The main tributaries are Cane Creek and Beard Cane Creek. Small streams with fishable water include: Hogan Hollow Creek (0.8 mile) and Bark Camp Run (0.5)

CANE CREEK

Location: Northwest section

Fishable miles: 2.0

Quad: Kinzel Springs, Blockhouse, Calderwood

Predominant species: Rainbow trout

Quality of fishing: Fair

Access: There are unmaintained trails either up Hesse Creek from Miller Cove to where it intersects Cane Creek Trail or from Cooper Road Trail, which begins at Abrams Creek Campground.

Beard Cane Creek

Fishable miles: 1.5

Quad: Kinzel Springs, Calderwood

Predominant species: Rainbow trout

Quality of fishing: Fair

Access: An unmaintained trail up Hesse Creek from Miller Cove intersects the Beard Cane Creek Trail 2.0 miles past Cane Creek, which follows the stream for its entire length. It is also accessible from Cooper Road Trail, which begins at Abrams Creek Campground.

PARSON BRANCH

Location: Western section

Fishable miles: 2.1

Quads: Calderwood, Tapoco

Predominant species: Rainbow trout

Quality of fishing: Fair to good

Access: The one-way Parsons Creek Road between Cades Cove and US 129 follows Parsons Creek for 2.1 miles before it leaves the park and empties into Calderwood Lake. Small streams with fishable water include: Bible Creek (1.9 miles) and Black Gum Branch (0.8).

GROUNDHOG CREEK

Location: Northeast section

Quad: Hartford

Predominant species: Rainbow trout

Quality of fishing: Good

Access: Groundhog Creek and two other streams, Robinson Creek and Rowdy Creek, that join it outside the park boundary, each offer nearly 2.0 miles of fishable water. They pass under TN 32 within a short distance of each other about midway between Cosby and Mt. Sterling, which hugs the park line.

COOPER CREEK

Location: South central section

Quads: Smokemont, Bryson City

Fishable miles: 2.9

Predominant species: Rainbow trout

Quality of fishing: Fair

Access: Drive to the end of Cooper Creek Road off NC 19 approximately 5.0 miles southwest of Cherokee. A sign marks the turn-off. The Cooper Creek Trail begins 0.4 mile from the end of the road, following the stream for nearly 2.0 miles. There is an unmaintained trail for the remainder of the fishable water.

Closed: Three streams that fit into this system are no longer available to fishermen: Dunn Creek, Indian Camp Creek, and Greenbriar Creek (Little Creek) are closed at the park boundary. Refer to the *Restricted Waters* map at the back of the book and the master list in chapter 2.

CONCLUSION

WHILE IT IS INEVITABLE THAT THE BATTLE AGAINST environmental and ecological problems will continue to be of major concern, Karen Wade, park superintendent, is optimistic regarding the future of the overall fishery.

> While we have seen an increase in fishing pressure over the years, we do not feel that the increase has had any significant impact on the long-term fish population in the park for two reasons. The success rate for most anglers is low, so whether we allow people to keep five fish, or three, or none at all would not dramatically affect the fishery. Our studies of large streams show little connection between fishing pressure and the fish population. What does drive these populations up or down are major natural events such as floods or prolonged drought.

Wade says that following the flooding in the spring of 1993, fish populations of both game and nongame species fell by up to 50 percent in the Little River while fishing pressure was extremely light due to restrictions on road access.

> Additionally, the mortality rate of trout from natural causes is high: 90 percent die within the first year; of the survivors, 40 to 50 percent die by the end of the second year; 70 to 80 percent die within the third year; and within the next year the mortality is essentially total. So for the most

part, anglers are taking home fish that would have died anyway of natural causes.

The Smokies streams have a large and avid following of anglers throughout the East, but it is not the opportunity to catch many or large trout that lures them back year after year. Instead, it is the environment of these splendid mountains, where it is always possible to find private places and an atmosphere that is manna for the soul.

Perhaps Robert Traver expressed this kind of obsession best in his heartwarming book *Anatomy of a Fisherman* (Peregrine Smith, Inc., 1978): "I love the environs where trout are found, which are invariably beautiful, and hate the environs where people are found, which are invariably ugly."

Anglers can find such environs in great abundance in the park because it is an ecological niche of enormous diversity. This is well documented in *The Sierra Club Guide to the National Parks of the East and Midwest,* which indicates that a trip from the base of the Smokies to Clingmans Dome would be the equivalent of a drive from Georgia to Maine. The lowest elevation in the park is 857 feet at the point where Abrams Creek empties into the Little Tennessee River, and the highest is 6,643 feet at Clingmans Dome, one of the sixteen peaks in the Smokies that reaches the 6,000-foot level.

From above the 4,500-foot level, the forest type is mostly Fraser fir and red spruce typical of Canadian woodlands; between 3,000 and 4,500 feet is a deciduous forest typical of the Great Lakes region and central New England. Below 3,000 feet are cove hardwoods of great size that flourish on the rich soil, and at the lowest elevations are the oaks and pines of the type found throughout the South. The changes are not

sharply defined; instead, the transitions are subtle and not easily detected.

So it is understandable why the Great Smoky Mountains
National Park casts a spell over fly fishermen of all ages: Within
its vastness are waters to satisfy anyone's desires or capabilities.
Just as important, being in this unique and intriguing atmosphere provides proof there are still wild and wonderful places
in which fly fishermen can enjoy their sport.

APPENDIX A

Backcountry Campsites

Please refer to the *Trail Map* at the end of the book.

CADES COVE AREA

Site No.	Rationed Capacity	Elev. (in feet)	Map Key
1 Cooper Road	(H)	1,200	2D
2 Cane Creek		1,360	2D
3 Hesse Creek	(H)	1,360	3D
4 Kelly Gap	(H)	1,930	3D
6 Turkey Pen Ridge		3,400	4D
7 Ace Gap	(H)	1,680	3C
9 Anthony Creek	(H)	3,200	4E
10 Ledbetter Ridge	(8, 8H)	3,000	4D
11 Beard Cane	(H)	1,530	2D
12 Forge Creek		2,600	3E
13 Sheep Pen Gap	(15, 8H)	4,640	2F
14 Flint Gap	(H)	2,050	2E
15 Rabbit Creek	(H)	1,550	2E
17 Little Bottoms		1,240	2D

ELKMONT/TREMONT AREA

Site No.	Rationed Capacity	Elev. (in feet)	Map Key
18 West Prong	(H)	1,600	4D
19 Upper Henderson	(H)	2,880	5D
20 King Branch	(H)	2,520	5D
21 Medicine Branch Bluff		3,780	6D

Site No.	Rationed Capacity	Elev. (in feet)	Map Key
23 Camp Rock	(12)	3,200	6D
24 Rough Creek	(15)	2,860	6D
25 Lower Buckeye Gap		3,540	6E
26 Dripping Spring Mt.		4,440	6D
27 Lower Jakes Gap	(H)	3,520	5D
28 Marks Cove	(H)	3,490	5D
30 Three Forks		3,400	6E

GREENBRIER/COSBY AREA

Site No.	Rationed Capacity	Elev. (in feet)	Map Key
29 Otter Creek	(10)	4,560	9C
31 Porters Flat		3,400	8D
32 Injun Creek		2,280	8C
33 Settlers Camp		1,960	9B
34 Sugar Cove		3,240	10B
35 Gilliland Creek	(H)	2,680	10B

CATALOOCHEE/BIG CREEK AREA

Site No.	Rationed Capacity	Elev. (in feet)	Map Key
36 U. Walnut Bottoms	(20, 20H)	3,040	11C
37 Lwr. Walnut Bottoms	(20)	3,000	11C
38 Mount Sterling	(12)	5,820	11C
39 Pretty Hollow	(H)	3,040	10B
40 Big Hemlock		3,100	11D
41 Caldwell Fork	(H)	3,360	11E
42 Spruce Mountain	(H)	5,480	10D

OCONALUFTEE AREA

Site No.	Rationed Capacity	Elev. (in feet)	Map Key
44 McGhee Spring	(H)	5,040	10D
47 Enloe Creek	(8)	3,620	10D
48 Upper Chasteen	Creek	3,320	9D
49 Cabin Flats	(H)	3,060	9D
50 Lwr. Chasteen	(15, 15H)	2,360	9E

DEEP CREEEK AREA

Site No.	Rationed Capacity	Elev. (in feet)	Map Key
52 Newton Bald	(H)	5,000	8E
53 Poke Patch		3,000	8E
54 Nettle Creek		2,600	8E
55 Pole Road	(15, 15H)	2,410	8E
56 Burnt Spruce	(H)	2,405	8F
57 Bryson Place	(20, 12H)	2,360	8F
58 Nicks Newst Branch	(H)	2,360	8F
59 McCracken Branch		2,320	7F
60 Bumgardner Branch	(H)	2,120	7F

NOLAND CREEK AREA

Site No.	Rationed Capacity	Elev. (in feet)	Map Key
61 Bald Creek	(12, 6H)	3,560	7E
62 Upper Ripskin	(H)	3,160	7F
63 Jerry Flats	(H)	2,920	7F
64 Mill Creek	(H)	2,540	7F
65 Bear Pen Branch	(H)	2,040	6F

Site No.	Rationed Capacity	Elev. (in feet)	Map Key
66 Lower Noland Creek		1,720	6G
67 Goldmine Branch	(H)	1,840	6G

FORNEY CREEK AREA

Site No.	Rationed Capacity	Elev. (in feet)	Map Key
68 Steel Trap		3,960	6E
69 Huggins		2,800	6F
70 Jonas Creek	(H)	2,400	6F
71 CCC	(12, 12H)	2,180	6F
73 Bear Creek	(H)	1,800	6F
74 Lower Forney		1,720	6G

HAZEL CREEK AREA

Site No.	Rationed Capacity	Elev. (in feet)	Map Key
81 North Shore	(H)	1,800	4G
82 Calhoun	(H)	2,720	5F
83 Bone Valley	(20, 10H)	2,280	5F
84 Sugar Fork		2,160	4F
85 Sawdust Pie	(H)	2,000	4F
86 Proctor	(H)	1,680	4F

TWENTYMILE AREA

Site No.	Rationed Capacity	Elev. (in feet)	Map Key
88 Pinnacle Creek	(H)	2,200	4F
89 Lower Ekaneetlee		1,880	4F

90 Lost Cove	(H)	1,760	3F
91 Upper Lost Cove	(H)	2,040	3F
92 Upper Flat	(H)	2,520	3F
93 Twentymile Creek		1,880	3F
95 Dalton Branch	(H)	2,360	2F
96 Eagle Creek Island		2,880	4F
97 Big Walnut		2,400	4E

CHAMBERS CREEK AREA

Site No.	Rationed Capacity	Elev. (in feet)	Map Key
75 Hicks Branch		1,720	5G
76 Kirkland Creek	(H)	1,770	5G
77 Pilkey Creek	(H)	1,800	5G
98 Chambers Creek	(H)	1,720	5G

SHELTERS

Shelter	Rationed Capacity	Elev. (in feet)	Map Key
Davenport Gap	(12, 12H)	2,600	11B
Cosby Knob	(12, 12H)	4,700	10C
Tricorner Knob	(12, 12H)	5,920	10C
Pecks Corner	(12, 12H)	5,280	9D
Icewater Spring	(12)	5,920	9D
Mt. Collins	(12)	5,870	7E
Double Spring Gap	(12)	5,507	6E
Silers Bald	(12, 12H)	5,460	6E
Derrick Knob	(12)	4,890	5E
Spence Field	(12, 12H)	4,900	4E
Russell Field	(14, 14H)	4,360	4E
Mollies Ridge	(12, 12H)	4,570	3E

Birch Spring Gap	(12, 12H)	3,680	3F
Mount LeConte	(12)	6,440	7D
Kephart	(14, 14H)	3,900	8D
Laurel Gap	(14, 14H)	5,600	10D
Rich Mountain	(8, 8H)	3,460	3D
Scott Gap	(8, 8H)	1,790	2E

APPENDIX B
Fly Hatch and Pattern Chart of the
Great Smoky Mountains National Park

JANUARY / FEBRUARY			

Hatches*

COMMON NAME	LATIN NAME	HOOK SIZE	TIME OF MONTH
Blue-Winged Olive	*Baetis vagans*	16 - 22	Sporadic Jan./All Feb.
Winter Black Stone	*Capnia vernalis*	18 - 22	All Jan./All Feb.
Little Black Stone	*Allocapnia aurora*	14 - 18	Mid to Late Feb.
Early Brown Stone	*Strophopteryx fasciata*	14 - 18	Mid to Late Feb.
Little Black Caddis	*Chimarra atterima*	16 - 18	Late Jan./All Feb.
Midges	*Dixella*	18 - 22	All Jan./All Feb.

FLY PATTERNS

Blue-Winged Olive	BWO (emerger, dry)	16 - 22
	Adams Para	16 - 22
	Hares Ear Nymph	16 - 22
Winter Black Stone	Lil Black Stone	18 - 22
	Black Caddis	18 - 22
	Black Stone Nymph	18
Little Black Stone	Lil Black Stone	14 - 18
	Black Caddis	14 - 18
	Black Stone Nymph	14 - 16
Early Brown Stone	Lil Brown Stone	14 - 18
	Tan Caddis	14 - 18
	Brown Stone Nymph	14 - 16
Little Black Caddis	Black Caddis	16 - 18
	Black Caddis Pupa	16 - 18
	Henryville	16 - 18
Midges	Griffiths Gnat	18 - 22
	Brassie	18 - 22

SUGGESTED ATTRACTOR PATTERNS

Wooly Buggers	Brown,Olive,Black	6 - 14
Muddler Minnow	Natural,White,Olive	6 - 14
Sculpin Minnow	Natural, Olive	6 - 14
Eggs	Pink, Orange	10 - 14

MARCH			

Hatches

COMMON NAME	LATIN NAME	HOOK SIZE	TIME OF MONTH
Blue-Winged Olive	*Baetis vagans*	16 - 18	All Month
Early Blue Quill	*Paraleptophlebia adoptiva*	16 - 18	All Month
Quill Gordan	*Epeorus pleuralis*	12 - 14	All Month

Little Black Stone	*Allocapnia aurora*	14 - 18	All Month
Early Brown Stone	*Strophopterex fasciata*	12 - 16	All Month
Hendrickson/Red Quill	*Ephemerella subvaria*	12 - 14	Late March
Dun Caddis	*Brachycentrus americanus*	14 - 18	All month
Midges	*Dixella*	18 - 22	All month

FLY PATTERNS

Blue-Winged Olive	BWO (emerger, dry)	16 - 18
	Adams Para	16 - 18
	Hares Ear Nymph	16 - 18
Early Blue Quill	Blue Quill	16 - 18
	Blue Dunn	16 - 18
	Adams Para	16 - 18
	Pheasant Tail Nymph	16 - 18
Quill Gordon	Quill Gordon	12 - 14
	Adams Para	12 - 14
Little Black Stone	Lil Black Stone	14 - 18
	Black Caddis	14 - 18
	Black Stone Nymph	14 - 16
Early Brown Stone	Lil Brown Stone	14 - 18
	Tan Caddis	14 - 18
	Brown Stone Nymph	14 - 16
Hendrickson/Red Quill	Hendrickson	12 - 14
	Red Quill	12 - 14
	Adams Dry	10 - 14
	Adams Para	12 - 14
	Pheasant Tail Nymph	14 - 16
	Hares Ear Nymph	14 - 16
Dun Caddis	Henryville	16 - 18
	Tan Caddis	16 - 18

SUGGESTED ATTRACTOR PATTERNS

Streamers:

Wooly Buggers	Brown, Olive, Black	6 - 14
Muddler Minnows	Natural, White, Olive	6 - 14
Sculpin Minnow	Natural, Olive	6 - 14

Dries:

Adams Dry		10 - 16
Adams Para		12 - 16
Female Adams		12 - 16
Thunderhead	Gray, Olive	12 - 16

Nymphs:

Bead-Head Hares Ear	14 - 18
Bead-Head Pheasant Tail	14 - 18
Bead-Head Prince Nymph	14

APRIL

Hatches

COMMON NAME	LATIN NAME	HOOK SIZE	TIME OF MONTH
Hendrickson/Red Quill	*Ephemerella subvaria*	12 - 14	All Month
Early Blue Quill	*Paraleptophlebia adoptiva*	16 - 18	All Month
Quill Gordan	*Epeorus pleuralis*	12 - 14	All Month
Blue-Winged Olive	*Baetis vagans*	16 - 18	Early April
March Brown	*Stenonema vicarium*	12 - 14	Mid to Late April
Gray Fox	*Stenonema ithaca*	12 - 14	Late April
Green Drake	*Ephemera guttulata*	8 - 12	Late April
Giant Black Stone	*Pteronarcys scotti*	6 - 12	All Month
Yellow Stone	*Isoperla bilineata*	12 -16	All Month
Green Caddis	*Rhyacophila lobifera*	14 - 18	Late April
Dun Caddis	*Brachycentrus americanus*	14 - 18	All Month
Light Cahill	*Stenonema ithaca*	14 - 16	Late April

FLY PATTERNS

Hendrickson/Red Quill	Hendrickson	12 - 14
	Red Quill	12 - 14
	Adams Dry	10 - 14
	Adams Para	12 - 14
	Pheasant Tail Nymph	14 - 16
	Hares Ear Nymph	14 - 16
Early Blue Quill	Blue Quill	16 - 18
	Blue Dun	16 - 18
	Adams Para	16 - 18
	Pheasant Tail Nymph	16 - 18
Quill Gordon	Quill Gordon	12 - 14
	Adams Para	12 - 14
Blue-Winged Olive	BWO (emerger, dry)	16 - 18
	Adams Para	16 - 18
	Hares Ear Nymph	16 - 18
March Brown	March Brown	12 - 14
	March Brown Nymph	12 - 14
Gray Fox	Gray Fox	14 - 16
	Adams Dry	14 - 16
	Hares Ear Nymph	14 - 16
Green Drake	Green Drake	8 - 10
	Coffin Fly	8 - 10
	Green Drake Spinner	8 - 10
Giant Black Stone	Black Stone Nymph	6 - 12
	Black Stimulator	6 - 12
Yellow Stone	Lil Yellow Stone	12 - 16
	Yellow Caddis	12 - 16
	Yellow Palmer	12 - 16
Green Caddis	Olive Caddis	16 - 18
Dun Caddis	Henryville	16 - 18
	Tan Caddis	16 - 18
Light Cahill	Light Cahill	12 - 16

Light Cahill Para		14 - 18
Light Cahill Nymph		14 - 16

SUGGESTED ATTRACTOR PATTERNS

Streamers:

Wooly Buggers	Brown, Olive, Black	6 - 14
Muddler Minnow	Natural, Black	6 - 14
Sculpin Minnow	Natural, Olive	6 - 14

Dries:

Adams Dry		10 - 16
Adams Para		12 - 16
Female Adams		12 - 16
Thunderhead	Gray, Olive	12 - 16
Adams Variant		12 - 14
Elk Wing Caddis	Gray, Tan, Olive, Yellow	12 - 18
Renegade		12 - 16
Porter's Caddis		12 - 16
Coffin Fly		8 - 12

Nymphs:

Bead-Head Hares Ear	12 - 16
Bead-Head Pheasant Tail	12 - 16
Bead-Head Zug Bug	12 - 16
Secret Weapon	12 - 16

MAY

Hatches

COMMON NAME	LATIN NAME	HOOK SIZE	TIME OF MONTH
Yellow Stone	*Isoperla bilineata*	14 - 16	All Month
March Brown	*Stenonema vicarium*	12 - 14	All Month
Maroon Drake	*Isonychia sadleri*	12 - 16	All Month Sporadic
Green Drake	*Ephemera guttulanta*	8 - 10	All Month Sporadic
Light Cahill	*Stenonema ithaca*	14 - 16	All Month
Rusty Spinner	*Baetis tricaudatus*	14 - 16	All Month
Gray Fox	*Stenonema ithaca*	12 - 14	All Month
Giant Black Stone	*Pteronarcys scotti*	6 - 12	All Month
Brown Stone	*Isoperla bilineata*	10 - 12	All Month
Dun Caddis	*Brachycentrus americanus*	14 - 16	All Month
Mottled Green Caddis	*Rhyacophila atrata*	12 - 14	All Month
Tiny Blue-Wing Olive	*Pseudocloeon anoka*	18 - 22	Late May
Sulphur Dun	*Ephemerella dorothea*	16 - 18	Late May
Midges	*Dixella*	18 - 22	All Month

FLY PATTERNS

Yellow Stone		
	Lil Yellow Stone	14 - 16
	Yellow Sally	14 - 16
	Yellow Caddis	14 - 16

	Yellow Palmer	14 - 16
March Brown	March Brown	12 - 14
	March Brown Nymph	12 - 14
	Ausable Wulff	12 - 14
Maroon Drake	Red Quill Body	12 - 16
Green Drake	Green Drake	8 - 10
	Green Drake Wulff	8 - 10
	Coffin Fly	8 - 10
Light Cahill	Light Cahill	12 - 16
	Light Cahill Para	12 - 16
	Light Cahill Nymph	14 - 16
Rusty Spinner	Rusty Wulff	14 - 16
	Orange Palmer	14 - 16
Gray Fox	Gray Fox	14 - 16
	Gray Wulff	14 - 16
	Adams Dry	14 - 16
	Hares Ear Nymph	14 - 16
Giant Black Stone	Black Stone Nymph	6 - 12
	Black Stimulator	6 - 12
Brown Stone	Brown Stone Nymph	10 - 12
Dun Caddis	Henryville	14 - 16
	Tan Caddis	14 - 16
Mottled Green Caddis	Olive Caddis	12 - 14
	Gray Caddis	12 - 14
Tiny Blue-Wing Olive	BWO (std. & para)	18 - 22
Sulphur Dun	Sulphur Dun	16 - 18
	Sulphur Para	16 - 18
	Sulphur Emerger	16 - 18

SUGGESTED ATTRACTOR PATTERNS
Streamers;

Wooly Buggers	Olive, Brown, Black	6 - 14
Micky Fin		8 - 14
Gray Ghost		8 - 14
Muddler Minnow	Natural	6 - 14

Dries:

Elk Wing Caddis	Olive, Tan, Gray, Black, Yellow, Orange, etc.	12 - 16
Adams Dry		10 - 16
Female Adams		12 - 16
Adams Para		12 - 18
Adams Variant		12 - 16
P. M. Para		12 - 16
Coffin Fly		8 - 12
Wulff's	Tennessee, Royal, Grizzly	12 - 16
Nelson's Caddis		12 - 14
Porter's Caddis		12 - 14

Nymphs:

Bead-Head Pheasant Tail	12 - 16
Bead- Head Hares Ear	12 - 16
Bead-Head Zug Bug	12 - 16
Tellico Nymph	12 - 14
Georges Nymph	12 - 16

JUNE

Hatches

COMMON NAME	LATIN NAME	HOOK SIZE	TIME OF MONTH
Light Cahill	*Stenonema ithaca*	12 - 16	All Month
Yellow Stone	*Isoperla bilineata*	12 - 16	All Month
Mottled Green Caddis	*Rhyacophila atrata*	12 - 14	All Month
Rusty Spinner	*Baetis tricaudatus*	14 - 16	All Month
Gray-Brown Caddis	*Brachycentrus spinae*	12 - 16	All Month
Gray Drake	*Siphlonurus occidentalis*	12 - 16	All Month
Sulphur Dun	*Ephemerella dorothea*	16 - 18	All Month
Leadwing Coachman	*Isonychia bicolor*	12 - 14	Mid to Late June
Giant Black Stone	*Pteronarcys scotti*	6 - 12	Early to Mid June
Brown Stone	*Isoperla bilineata*	10 - 12	All Month
Yellow Caddis	*Hydropsyche carolina*	14 - 18	Late June
Midges	*Dixella*	18 - 22	All Month
Terrestrials*			All Month

FLY PATTERNS

Light Cahill	Light Cahill	12 - 16
	Light Cahill Para	12 - 16
	Light Cahill Nymph	12 - 16
Yellow Stone	Lil Yellow Stone	12 - 16
	Yellow Sally	12 - 16
	Yellow Caddis	12 - 16
	Yellow Stimulator	12 - 16
Mottled Green Caddis	Olive Caddis	12 - 14
Rusty Spinner	Rusty Wulff	14 - 16
	Orange Palmer	14 - 16
Gray-Brown Caddis	Gray Caddis	12 - 16
	Brown Caddis	12 - 16
Gray Drake	Gray Wulff	12 - 16
	Adams Dry	12 - 16
	Hares Ear Nymph	12 - 16
Sulphur Dun	Sulphur Dun	16 - 18
	Sulphur Para	16 - 18
Leadwing Coachman	Leadwing Coachman	12 - 14
	Adams Dry	12 - 14
	Pheasant Tail Nymph	12 - 16
Giant Black Stone	Black Stone Nymph	6 - 12
	Black Stimulator	6 - 12
Brown Stone	Brown Stone Nymph	10 - 12

Yellow Caddis	Yellow Caddis	14 - 18
Terrestrials	Hoppers	12 - 14
	Ants	16 - 18
	Inchworms	10 - 14

SUGGESTED ATTRACTOR PATTERNS
Dries:

Elk Wing Caddis	All Colors	12 - 16
Adams Dry		10 - 16
Adams Para		12 - 16
Adams Variant		12 - 16
P.M. Para		12 - 14
Wulff's	Tennessee, Royal, Grizzly	12 - 16
Humpies	Fl. Green, Red, Yellow	12 - 16
Nelson's Caddis		12 - 14
Porter's Caddis		12 - 14
Renegade		12 - 14
Palmers	Fl. Green, Yellow	12 - 14

Nymphs:

Bead-Head Pheasant Tail		12 - 16
Bead-Head Hares Ear		12 - 16
Bead-Head Zug Bug		12 - 16
Tellico Nymph		12 - 14
Georges Nymph		12 - 16

JULY / AUGUST

Hatches

COMMON NAME	LATIN NAME	HOOK SIZE	TIME OF MONTH
Light Cahill	*Stenonema ithaca*	14 - 16	All July/All August
Leadwing Coachman	*Isonychnia bicolor*	10 - 14	All July/All August
Rusty Spinner	*Baetis tricaudatus*	14 - 16	All July/All August
Yellow Stone	*Isoperla bilineata*	12 - 16	All July/All August
Dun Caddis	*Brachycentrus americanus*	16 - 18	All July/All August
Gray-Brown Caddis	*Brachycentrus spinae*	12 - 16	All July/All August
Mottled Green Caddis	*Rhyacophila atrata*	10 - 14	All July All August
Tan Caddis	*Heteroplectron americanum*	14 - 18	All July All August
Brown Stone	*Isoperla bilineata*	10 - 12	All July
Little Dark Olive	*Siphlonurus rapidus*	16 - 18	Late July All August
Black Spinner	*Tricorythodes*	14 - 20	All August
Yellow Caddis	*Hydropsyche carolina*	14 - 18	All July/Early August
Midges	*Dixella*	18 - 22	All July/All August
Terrestrials			All July/ All August

FLY PATTERNS

Light Cahill	Light Cahill	14 - 16
	Light Cahill Para	14 - 16
	Light Cahill Nymph	12 - 16

Leadwing Coachman	Leadwing Coachman	10 - 14
	Adams Dry	10 - 14
	Pheasant Tail Nymph	12 - 16
Rusty Spinner	Rusty Wulff	14 - 16
	Rusty Wulff Para	14 - 16
	Orange Palmer	14 - 16
Yellow Stone	Lil Yellow Stone	12 - 16
	Yellow Sally	12 - 16
	Yellow Caddis	12 - 16
	Yellow Stimulator	12 - 16
Dun Caddis	Henryville	16 - 18
Gray-Brown Caddis	Gray Caddis	12 - 16
	Brown Caddis	12 - 16
Mottled Green Caddis	Olive Caddis	12 - 16
	Female Caddis	12 - 16
Tan Caddis	Tan Caddis	14 - 18
Brown Stone	Brown Stone Nymph	10 - 12
Little Dark Olive	BWO (dry, para, emerger)	16 - 18
Black Spinner	Black Spinner	10 - 14
	Black Adams	10 - 14
	Don's Pet	10 - 14
Yellow Caddis	Yellow Caddis	14 - 16
	Chartreuse Caddis	14 - 16
Terrestrials	Hoppers	8 - 14
	Ants	16 - 18
	Inchworms	10 - 14
	Beetles	12 - 16
	Bees	10 - 16

SUGGESTED ATTRACTOR PATTERNS
Dries:

Elk Wing Caddis	All Colors (Esp. Bright)	12 - 16
Adams Dry		10 - 16
Adams Para		12 - 18
P.M. Para		12 - 16
Wulff's	Tennessee, Royal, Grizzly	12 - 16
Porter's Caddis		12 - 16
Renegade		12 - 16
Humpies	Fl. Green, Red, Yellow	12 - 16
Stimulator	Olive, Orange, Red, Yellow	10 - 14
Palmers	Fl. Green, Yellow	12 - 14

Nymphs:

Bead-Head Prince		12 - 16
Bead-Head Hares Ear		12 - 16
Bead-Head Pheasant Tail		12 - 16
Tellico		10 - 16
Georges Nymph		12 - 16

SEPTEMBER

Hatches

COMMON NAME	LATIN NAME	HOOK SIZE	TIME OF MONTH
Light Cahill	*Stenonema ithaca*	14 - 16	Early September
Leadwing Coachman	*Isoychnia bicolor*	10 - 14	Early Septemner
Black Spinner	*Trichorythodes*	10 - 14	All Month
Rusty Spinner	*Baetis tricaudatus*	14 - 16	Early September
Yellow Stone	*Isoperla bilineata*	12 - 16	Early September
Giant Tan Caddis	*Heteroplectron*	8 - 10	All September
Yellow Caddis	*Hydropsyche carolina*	14 - 18	All September
Little Dark olive	*Siphlonurus rapidus*	16 - 18	All September
Midges	*Dixella*	18 - 22	All Month
Terrestrials			All Month

FLY PATTERNS

Light Cahill	Light Cahill	12 - 16
	Light Cahill Para	12 - 16
	Light cahill Nymph	12 - 16
Leadwing Coachman	Leadwing coachman	10 - 14
	Adams Dry	10 - 14
	Adams Para	12 - 14
	Pheasant Tail nymph	12 - 16
Black Spinner	Black Spinner	10 - 14
	Adams Para	10 - 14
	Don's Pet	10 - 14
Rusty Spinner	Rusty Wulff	14 - 16
	Orange Palmer	14 - 16
Yellow Stone	Lil Yellow Stone	12 - 16
	Yellow Sally	12 - 16
	Yellow Caddis	12 - 16
Giant Tan Caddis	Tan Caddis	8 - 12
	Tan Pupa	8 - 12
Yellow Caddis	Yellow Caddis	12 - 16
	Chatreuse Caddis	12 - 16
Little Dark Olive	BWO(dry, para, emerger)	16 - 18
Terrestrials	Hoppers (olive)	8 - 14
	Ants	16 - 18
	Inchworm	10 - 14
	Bees	8 - 14
	Beetles	12 - 16

SUGGESTED ATTRACTOR PATTERNS

Dries:

Adams Dry		10 - 16
Adams Para		10 - 16
Adams Female		12 - 14
P.M. Para		12 - 14
Palmers	Orange, Yellow, Lime	12 - 14
Humpies	Fl. Green, Red, Yellow	12 - 14

| Nelson's Caddis | 12 - 14 |
| Porter's Caddis | 12 - 14 |

Nymphs:

Bead-Head Pheasant Tail	12 - 16
Bead-Head Hares Ear	12 - 16
Tellico	8 - 16

OCTOBER / NOVEMBER

Hatches

COMMON NAME	LATIN NAME	HOOK SIZE	TIME OF MONTH
Blue-Winged Olive	*Baetis vagans*	16 - 18	All Oct./All Nov.
Dun Caddis	*Brachycentrus americanus*	16 - 20	All Oct./All Nov.
Little Dark Olive	*Siphlonurus rapidus*	18 - 22	All Oct. to Mid Nov.
Blue Quill	*Paraleptophlebia adoptiva*	16 - 18	All Oct./All Nov.
Giant Tan Caddis	*Heteroplectron*	8 - 10	All Oct. to Early Nov.
Yellow Caddis	*Hydropsyche carolina*	14 - 18	All Oct. to Mid Nov.
Midges	*Dixella*	18 - 22	All Oct./All Nov.

FLY PATTERNS

Blue-Winged Olive	BWO (dry, para, emerger)	16 - 18
	Adams Para	16 - 18
	Hares Ear Nymph	14 - 18
	Pheasant Tail Nymph	14 - 18
Dun Caddis	Henryville	16 - 18
Little Dark Olive	BWO Para	18 - 22
	BWO Emerger	18
Blue Quill	Blue Quill	14 - 18
	Blue Dun	14 - 18
	Blue Dun Para	14 - 20
	Pheasant Tail Nymph	14 - 18
Giant Tan Caddis	Tan Caddis	8 - 10
	Tan Stimulator	8 - 10
	Tan Pupa	8 - 10
Yellow Caddis	Yellow Caddis	14 - 18
	Green Pupa	12 - 16
Midges	Grifiths Gnat	18 - 22
	Adams Para	18 - 22
	Brassie	18

SUGGESTED ATTRACTOR PATTERNS

Streamers:

Wooly Buggers	Olive, Brown, Black	6 - 14
Muddler Minnows	Natural, Black	6 - 14
Black Ghost		6 - 12

Dries:

Adams		14 - 22
Adams Para		16 - 22
Palmer, Orange		12 - 16
Elk-Wing Caddis		12 - 18
P.M. Para		12 - 16

Nymphs:

Bead Heads		12 - 18
Stone Fly Nymphs	Dark	6 - 12
Tellico	Olive	6 - 10

DECEMBER

Hatches

COMMON NAME	LATIN NAME	HOOK SIZE	TIME OF MONTH
Blue-Winged Olive	*Baetis vagans*	18 - 22	All December
Winter Black Stone	*Capnia vernalis*	18 - 22	All December
Midges	*Dixella*	18 - 22	All December
Blue Quill	*Paraleptophlebia adoptiva*	16 - 18	Early December

FLY PATTERNS

Blue-Winged Olive	BWO (dry, para, emerger)	18 - 22
	Adams Para	18
Winter Black Stone	Lil Black Stone	16 - 22
Midges	Griffiths Gnat	18 - 22
	Adams Para	18 - 22
	Brassie	18
Blue Quill	Blue Quill	16 - 18
	Blue Dun	16 - 18

SUGGESTED ATTRACTOR PATTERNS

Streamers:

Wooly Buggers	Olive, Black, Brown	6 - 10
Black Ghost		6 - 10
Muddler Minnow	Natural	6 - 12

Dries:

Adams Para		16 - 22
Blue Dun Para		16 - 22

Nymphs:

Bead-Head Nymphs		14 - 18
Big Stone Nymphs	Black, Brown	6 - 12

*Denotes a time of year, both photoperiod and temperature, in which little insect activity is documented. Hatches are very sporadic and often occur during warmer, overcast, and drizzly days.

Author H. Lea Lawrence gears up for an afternoon of his favorite activity.

ABOUT THE AUTHOR

A freelance writer for over thirty years, H. Lea Lawrence has been published in more than fifty outdoor, nature, scientific, and general interest magazines. *The Fly Fisherman's Guide to the Great Smoky Mountains National Park* is his sixth book. Lawrence lives in Franklin, Tennessee.

MAPS

The maps on the following pages can also be accessed digitally at: https://turnerbookstore.com/products/fly-fishermans-guide-to-the-great-smoky-mountains-national-park

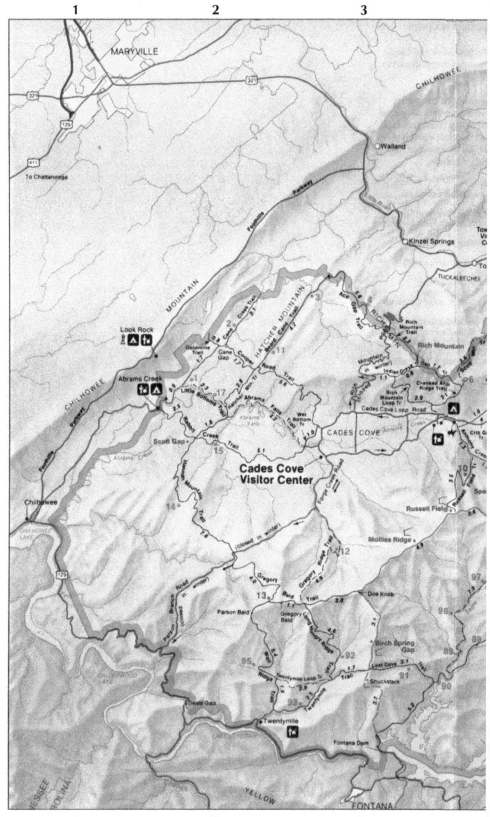

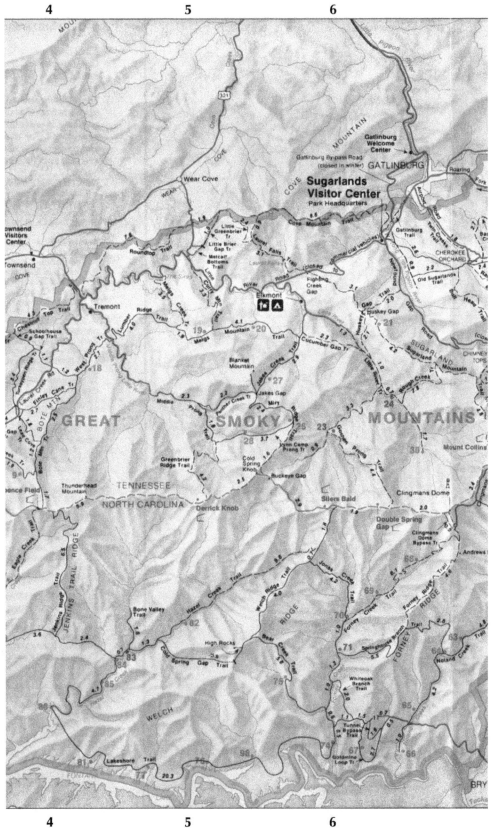

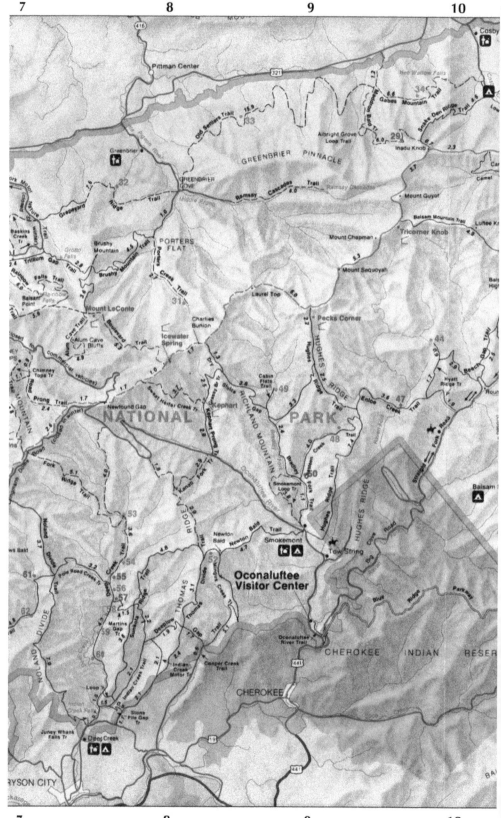

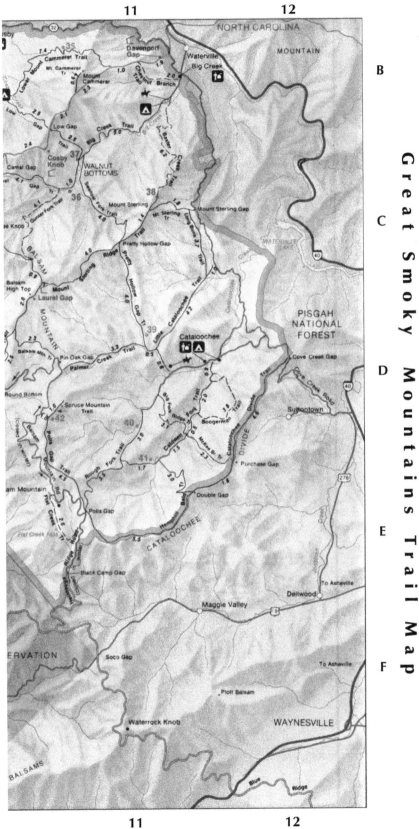

Restricted Waters

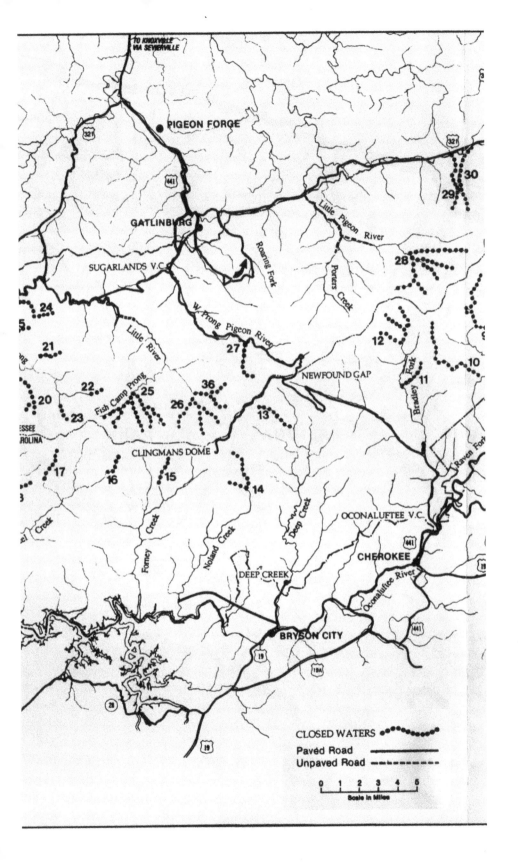

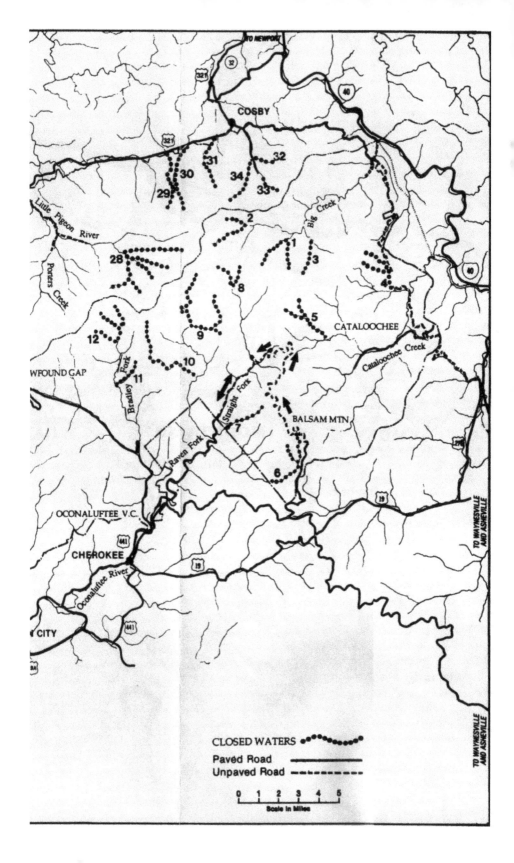

CLOSED AND EXCLUDED WATERS

All of the waters of Mingus Creek and Lands Creek are public water supplies and closed to fishing.

The following streams and their tributaries upstream from the points described are closed to fishing, in order that native brook trout can be protected. For exact location, consult the appropriate USGS 1:24,000 Quadrangle Map available at all Park visitor centers.

NORTH CAROLINA
1. Gunter Cr. at the first trail crossing on Gunter at 3240' elev.
2. Big Cr. and Yellow Cr. at their junction.
3. McGinty Cr. at its confluence with Swallow Fork.
4. Correll Br. at the junction with Litte Cataloochee Cr.
5. Lost Bottom Cr. at its confluence with Palmer Cr. at 3280' elev.
6. Bunches Cr. at the Park boundary.
7. Stillwell Cr. at the Park boundary.
8. Straight Fork and Balsam Corner Creek at their common junction.
9. Raven Fork at Big Pool which is the confluence of Left Fork, Middle Fork and Right Fork (also known as Three Forks).
10. Enloe Cr. at the junction with Raven Fork.
11. Taywa Cr. at its confluence with Bradley Fork.
12. Chasm Prong and Gulf Prong at their common junction on Bradley Fork.
13. Sahlee Cr. at its confluence with Deep Cr.
14. Noland Cr. and Salola Br. at their confluence.
15. Huggins Cr. (tributaary of Forney Cr.) at the cascade at 3700' elev.
16. Hazel Cr. at the cascades.
17. Walkers Cr. at the falls at 3400' elev.
18. Defeat Br. at its juntion with Bone Valley Cr.
19. Gunna Cr. (tributary to Eagle Cr.) at trail crossing at 3080' elev.

TENNESSEE
20. Sams Cr. at the confluence with Thunderhead Prong
21. Marks Creek at the falls at 2600'.
22. Lynn Camp Prong at campsite #28 (Mark's Cover).
23. Indian Flats Prong at the Middle Prong trail crossing.
24. Meigs Cr. at its confluence with Little R.
25. Fish Camp Prong and Goshen Cr. at their common junction.
26. Little R. and Grouse Cr. at their common junction.
27. Road Prong at its confluence with West Prong of Little Pigeon R.
28. Buck Fork and Middle Prong of the Little Pigeon R. at their common junction.
29. Dunn Cr. at Park boundary.
30. Indian Camp Cr. at Park boundary.
31. Greenbrier Cr. (Little Cr.) at Park boundary.
32. Toms Cr. at its junction with Cosby Cr.
33. Cosby Cr. where Low Gap Trail crosses the stream.
34. Rock Cr. at its junction with Cosby Cr.
35. Spruce Flats Cr. at its confluence with Middle Prong of Little R.
36. Meigs Post Prong at its confluence with Little R.